5G CONCEPTS AND APPLICATIONS

5G CONCEPTS AND APPLICATIONS

Aishwarya D. | Abirami R.

KHANNA BOOK PUBLISHING CO. (P) Ltd.
4C/4344, Ansari Road, Darya Ganj, New Delhi, India

Sathyabama Institute of Science and Technology
Jeppiaar Nagar, Rajiv Gandhi Salai, Chennai, Tamilnadu, India

Dear Readers,

To prevent the piracy, this book is secured with HIGH SECURITY HOLOGRAM on the front title cover. In case you don't find the hologram on the front cover title, please write us to at contact@khannabooks.com or whatsapp us at +91-99109 09320 and avail special gift voucher for yourself.

Specimen of Hologram on front Cover title:

Moreover, there is a SPECIAL DISCOUNT COUPON for you with EVERY HOLOGRAM.

How to avail this SPECIAL DISCOUNT:

Step 1: Scratch the hologram
Step 2: Under the scratch area, your "coupon code" is available
Step 3: Logon to www.khannabooks.com
Step 4: Use your "coupon code" in the shopping cart and get your copy at a special discount
Step 5: Enjoy your reading!

Thanks,
Khanna Publishing House

ISBN: 978-93-55384-43-0

5G Concepts and Applications
by **Aishwarya D.; Abirami R.**

First Edition: 2025

To view complete list of books, please scan the QR Code:

Published by:
Khanna Book Publishing Co. (P) Ltd.
CIN: U22110DL1998PTC095547

Visit us at: www.khannabooks.com
Write us at: contact@khannabooks.com

Printed in Bharat.

Preface

The evolution of wireless communication has been a defining force in shaping modern society. From the early days of 1G, which introduced mobile voice calls, to the high-speed data capabilities of 4G, each generation has pushed the boundaries of connectivity. Now, we stand at the threshold of a new era with 5G technology, a revolutionary leap that promises ultra-fast speeds, low latency, and massive network capacity.

5G is not merely an upgrade to its predecessor but a transformative technology that will power smart cities, autonomous vehicles, the Internet of Things (IoT), and next-generation applications in healthcare, education, and industry. It is set to redefine how we interact with the digital world, enabling seamless communication, real-time decision-making, and unprecedented levels of automation.

This book delves into the core aspects of 5G technology, including its architecture, benefits, challenges, and potential impact across various sectors. Whether you are a student, a researcher, a professional, or an enthusiast, this exploration of 5G will provide valuable insights into the future of connectivity and its role in driving global digital transformation.

As we embrace this technological advancement, it is essential to understand its implications, opportunities, and the responsibilities that come with it. The journey toward a fully connected world has begun, and 5G is at its forefront.

Aishwarya D.
Abirami R.

Contents

1 Overview of Mobile Communication Generation

Outcome

- **Evolution from Analog to Digital:** Mobile communication has transitioned from analog (1G) to digital (2G-5G), improving efficiency, security, and speed.
- **Global Connectivity:** Mobile networks have connected billions of people worldwide, bridging communication gaps and enabling instant access to information.
- **Impact on Society and Business:** Mobile communication has transformed education, healthcare, e-commerce, and social interactions, making remote work and online learning possible.
- **Introduction of Wireless Data Services:** From SMS and MMS in 2G to video streaming and IoT in 5G, mobile communication has enabled a data-driven digital world.
- **Future of Mobile Communication (6G & Beyond):** Emerging technologies like 6G, AI-powered communication, and satellite internet will further enhance speed, efficiency, and global accessibility.

1.1 INTRODUCTION TO WIRELESS COMMUNICATION

Wireless communication is the transmission of information without the need for physical cables or wires. It enables the exchange of data over distances using electromagnetic waves, such as radio, microwave, and infrared signals. The evolution of wireless communication has transformed how people connect, from early radio transmissions to modern high-speed mobile networks. Starting with 1G (analog voice calls), the technology has advanced through 2G (digital voice and SMS), 3G (mobile internet), 4G (high-speed data and streaming), and now 5G (ultra-fast, low-latency communication). Wireless communication powers everyday applications, including mobile phones, Wi-Fi, Bluetooth, satellite communication, and the Internet of Things (IoT). As technology advances, wireless networks continue to become faster, more efficient, and capable of handling massive amounts of connected devices, shaping the future of communication and digital connectivity.

1.1.1 Overview of Mobile Communication

Mobile communication refers to the technology that allows users to communicate wirelessly while moving, without being restricted to a fixed location. It enables voice calls, messaging, internet access, and multimedia transmission through mobile devices like smartphones, tablets, and laptops. The evolution of mobile communication has gone through several generations:

- **1G (First Generation):** Introduced in the 1980s, it used **analog signals** for voice calls but had poor sound quality and security.

- **2G (Second Generation):** Launched in the 1990s, it introduced **digital transmission**, enabling SMS, MMS, and basic internet services.
- **3G (Third Generation):** Early 2000s technology that provided **higher data speeds**, supporting video calls, mobile internet, and streaming.
- **4G (Fourth Generation):** Introduced in the 2010s, it brought **high-speed broadband**, making HD video streaming, VoIP, and online gaming seamless.
- **5G (Fifth Generation):** The latest advancement, offering **ultra-fast speeds, low latency, and massive device connectivity**, transforming industries such as healthcare, autonomous vehicles, and smart cities.

Mobile communication relies on **cellular networks**, where areas are divided into "cells," each served by a base station (cell tower). These networks use different frequency bands and protocols to ensure seamless connectivity as users move from one location to another. Technologies like **Wi-Fi, Bluetooth, and satellite communication** also play a role in expanding wireless connectivity beyond traditional mobile networks.

The First Mobile Call: The first-ever mobile phone call was made on April 3, 1973 by Martin Cooper, an engineer at Motorola. He called a rival at Bell Labs using a prototype of the Motorola DynaTAC 8000X.

Interesting Fact

With continuous innovation, mobile communication is evolving toward **6G**, which is expected to integrate **AI, advanced IoT, and terahertz waves** for even faster and more efficient connectivity in the future.

1.2 EVOLUTION OF 5G: THE ROAD TO 5G: EVOLUTION FROM 1G TO 4G

The journey to **5G (Fifth Generation)** mobile communication has been shaped by decades of technological advancements, each generation improving upon the last in terms of speed, capacity, and efficiency. This chapter will explore the evolution of 5G, starting from the early days of mobile communication and progressing through the key innovations that led to the development of this revolutionary technology.

1.2.1 1G – The Beginning of Mobile Communication (1980s)

The **first generation** (1G) of mobile communication, introduced in the **1980s**, was based on **analog technology**. It allowed for basic voice calls but suffered from poor sound quality, limited coverage, low security, and a lack of data services. Some key features of 1G included:

- Analog signal transmission
- Large, bulky mobile phones
- High call drop rates and interference
- No encryption, making calls easy to intercept

1.2.2 2G – The Digital Revolution (1990s)

The **second generation (2G)**, introduced in the early **1990s**, was a major breakthrough because it transitioned from **analog to digital communication**. This shift improved call quality, security, and efficiency while enabling new services such as:

- **Short Message Service** (SMS) and **Multimedia Messaging Service** (MMS)
- Better voice quality and reduced interference
- **GSM (Global System for Mobile Communications)** became the standard
- Introduction of basic mobile internet services with **GPRS (2.5G)** and **EDGE (2.75G)**

1.2.3 3G – The Era of Mobile Internet (2000s)

With the rise of the internet, the **third generation** (3G) networks were developed in the **2000s** to support **high speed data transmission** and more advanced applications, including:

- Faster internet speeds (up to **2 Mbps**)
- Mobile web browsing, email, and social media
- **Video calls** and early streaming services
- **Introduction of UMTS (Universal Mobile Telecommunications System)** and **HSPA (High-Speed Packet Access)**

1.2.4 4G – The Age of High-Speed Broadband (2010s)

The **fourth generation** (4G) revolutionized mobile communication by delivering **high-speed broadband connectivity**, enabling seamless streaming, online gaming, and advanced applications. Key advancements included:

- **Speeds up to 100 Mbps - 1 Gbps** (ideal for HD video streaming and VoIP calls)
- **LTE (Long-Term Evolution)** became the dominant 4G technology
- **Improved spectrum efficiency** and lower latency
- **Rise of mobile apps, cloud computing, and the Internet of Things (IoT)**

However, as digital transformation accelerated, 4G networks began facing limitations in handling massive data traffic, device connectivity, and latency-sensitive applications. This led to the development of 5G.

1.2.5 The Birth of 5G: A New Era of Connectivity

The demand for **faster, more reliable, and efficient networks** led to the creation of **5G**, which officially started rolling out in the **late 2010s and early 2020s**. It was designed to address the shortcomings of previous generations and introduce revolutionary features such as:

- **Ultra-fast speeds** (Up to **10 Gbps**, nearly **100 times faster than 4G**)
- **Ultra-low latency** (as low as **1 millisecond**, enabling real-time applications)
- **Massive connectivity** (can support **millions of devices per square kilometer**)
- **Improved energy efficiency** and **network slicing** for optimized performance
- **Support for emerging technologies** like autonomous vehicles, smart cities, and augmented reality (AR)

To achieve these improvements, 5G relies on **advanced technologies** such as:

- **Millimeter Waves (mmWave):** Uses high-frequency bands for faster speeds
- **Massive MIMO (Multiple Input, Multiple Output):** Increases network capacity and efficiency
- **Beamforming:** Directs signals more precisely to improve coverage and speed
- **Edge Computing:** Reduces latency by processing data closer to users

1.2.6 The Future Beyond 5G: Towards 6G

While **5G** is still being deployed worldwide, research has already begun on **6G**, which is expected to be introduced in the **2030s**. Future wireless communication will likely integrate:

- **Artificial Intelligence (AI)-powered networks**
- **Terahertz (THz) frequencies** for even higher speeds
- **Fully immersive AR/VR experiences**
- **Holographic communication** and advanced quantum computing applications

The evolution from **1G to 5G** has drastically transformed how people communicate, work, and interact with technology. As 5G continues to expand, it will unlock **new possibilities in industries such as healthcare, transportation, and smart infrastructure**, paving the way for an even more connected future.

> There are currently more mobile phone subscriptions in the world than there are people! The number of active mobile connections exceeded the global population years ago.
>
> **Did You Know**

This chapter provides a comprehensive look at how mobile communication has evolved over the decades, leading to the development of **5G** and beyond.

1.3 FROM MOBILE BROADBAND (MBB) TO EXTREME MOBILE BROADBAND (EMBB)

As mobile communication technology has evolved, the demand for **faster, more reliable, and data-intensive services** has grown exponentially. This shift has led to the transition from traditional **Mobile Broadband (MBB)** to **Extreme Mobile Broadband (eMBB)** in the 5G era, enabling ultra-high-speed connectivity for applications like **4K/8K video streaming, virtual reality (VR), and cloud gaming**. This chapter explores the evolution, key differences, and impact of eMBB in transforming mobile experiences.

1.3.1 Understanding Mobile Broadband (MBB)

Mobile Broadband (MBB) refers to high-speed wireless internet access delivered through cellular networks. It allows users to browse the internet, stream content, use social media, and access cloud-based applications on mobile devices.

Evolution of Mobile Broadband

Mobile broadband has evolved through different generations of wireless technology:

- **3G MBB**: The first real mobile broadband experience, enabling basic web browsing, video calling, and app usage.
- **4G LTE MBB**: Enhanced speeds (up to **100 Mbps**), enabling HD video streaming, VoIP calls, and faster downloads.
- **5G eMBB (Extreme Mobile Broadband)**: A revolutionary upgrade, offering speeds up to **10 Gbps**, ultra-low latency, and high network capacity for next-generation applications.

Extreme Mobile Broadband (eMBB) is a core feature of **5G networks**, designed to deliver **exceptionally high data rates, seamless connectivity, and superior user experiences**. It extends beyond traditional MBB by supporting bandwidth-intensive applications, immersive technologies, and ultra-fast wireless access in crowded areas.

Key Features of eMBB

- **Ultra-fast Speeds:** Up to **10 Gbps**, enabling real-time streaming of **4K/8K videos, VR, and AR applications**.
- **Low Latency:** Response times as low as **1 millisecond (ms)** for smooth interactions in gaming and video calls.
- **High Capacity:** Supports millions of devices simultaneously in dense urban areas, stadiums, and event venues.
- **Reliable Connectivity:** Maintains stable connections even in high-speed mobility scenarios (e.g., on trains or in cars).

1.3.2 Applications of Extreme Mobile Broadband

1. **Ultra-HD Streaming & Cloud-Based Entertainment**
   - **4K/8K Video Streaming:** High-quality, buffer-free streaming on mobile devices.
   - **Cloud Gaming (e.g., Google Stadia, Xbox Cloud Gaming):** Enables gaming without the need for powerful local hardware.
2. **Immersive Technologies Virtual Reality (VR) & Augmented Reality (AR)**
   - **VR/AR in Gaming:** Enhanced real-time experiences in the metaverse and multiplayer gaming.
   - **Remote Collaboration:** Virtual meetings with **holographic displays and 3D interactions.**
3. **Smart Cities & Transportation**
   - **Autonomous Vehicles:** High-speed communication between cars and infrastructure.
   - **Smart Public Transport:** High-speed Wi-Fi and seamless connectivity in buses, trains, and airports.
4. **Industrial & Healthcare Innovations**
   - **Remote Surgeries & Telemedicine:** Real-time, high-quality video interactions for remote healthcare.
   - **Smart Factories:** Cloud-controlled robotics and automation using ultra-fast wireless networks.

1.3.3 The Technologies Behind eMBB

To achieve the goals of **Extreme Mobile Broadband**, 5G networks rely on several key technologies:

1. **Millimeter-Wave (mmWave) Spectrum**
   - Uses **high-frequency bands (24 GHz to 100 GHz)** to deliver ultra-high speeds.
   - Ideal for urban areas, stadiums, and high-traffic locations.
2. **Massive MIMO (Multiple Input, Multiple Output)**
   - Uses multiple antennas to **boost data rates and increase capacity**.
   - Allows multiple users to access high-speed internet simultaneously.

3. Beamforming & Network Slicing

- **Beamforming**: Directs signals precisely toward users for improved connectivity.
- **Network Slicing**: Creates virtual networks optimized for specific applications (e.g., dedicated slices for VR gaming).

1.3.4 Challenges and Future of eMBB and Future Developments

While **eMBB** brings revolutionary improvements, it also comes with challenges:

- **Infrastructure Costs:** Requires extensive deployment of **5G small cells and fiber optic networks**.
- **Device Compatibility:** Older smartphones and devices do not support **mmWave** and **advanced 5G features**.
- **Energy Consumption:** Higher data speeds lead to increased power usage, requiring **energy-efficient solutions**.

Looking ahead, **6G networks** will take eMBB even further, offering:

- **Speeds exceeding 100 Gbps** with ultra-low latency.
- **AI-driven network optimizations** for improved efficiency.
- **Integration of terahertz (THz) frequencies** for next-level wireless experiences.

The transition from **Mobile Broadband (MBB) to Extreme Mobile Broadband (eMBB)** represents a significant leap in wireless communication. With **unprecedented speeds, ultra-low latency, and massive capacity**, eMBB is unlocking new possibilities in **entertainment, business, healthcare, and smart infrastructure**. As 5G continues to expand globally, **eMBB will shape the future of connectivity**, bringing us closer to a fully digital and immersive world.

The Fastest Mobile Network Recorded Over 10 Gbps. 5G networks have achieved speeds of over 10 Gbps, which is faster than most home WiFi connections.

Facts

1.4 THE RELATIONSHIP BETWEEN IOT AND 5G TECHNOLOGY

The **Internet of Things (IoT)** is transforming the way we interact with the digital world by enabling smart devices, sensors, and machines to communicate and share data seamlessly. As IoT expands, it requires a **high-speed, low-latency, and highly efficient network** to support millions of connected devices. This is where **5G technology** plays a crucial role.

5G is designed to meet the unique demands of IoT by offering **ultra-fast connectivity, massive device support, and improved energy efficiency**. Unlike previous generations of mobile networks, 5G can **handle a vast number of simultaneous connections**, making it ideal for IoT applications in industries such as **smart cities, healthcare, autonomous vehicles, industrial automation, and agriculture**.

This chapter explores how **5G and IoT** are interconnected, their combined impact on different sectors, and how this relationship will shape the future of digital transformation.

1.4.1 Understanding IoT and Its Growth

The **Internet of Things (IoT)** refers to a network of **smart devices, sensors, and machines** that collect, transmit, and analyze data through the internet. These devices range from **smart home gadgets (like thermostats and security cameras) to industrial automation systems, connected vehicles, and medical monitoring devices**. With advancements in cloud computing, AI, and edge computing, the number of IoT devices is growing rapidly. Experts estimate that by **2030, over 50 billion IoT devices** will be connected worldwide, requiring a **robust and scalable communication network** like 5G.

1.4.2. How 5G Enhances IoT Capabilities

1. Ultra-Low Latency for Real-Time Applications

- 5G reduces latency to as low as **1 millisecond (ms)**, enabling **real-time responses** in applications like autonomous vehicles, remote surgeries, and industrial robotics.
- **Example:** A **self-driving car** can instantly react to traffic conditions and obstacles due to real-time data processing enabled by 5G.

2. Massive IoT Connectivity

- 5G supports up to **1 million connected devices per square kilometer**, making it ideal for large-scale IoT deployments in **smart cities, smart factories, and agriculture**.
- **Example:** In a **smart city**, 5G can connect **traffic sensors, surveillance cameras, waste management systems, and environmental monitors** simultaneously.

3. High-Speed Data Transfer

- With speeds up to **10 Gbps**, 5G allows IoT devices to send and receive large amounts of data instantly.
- **Example: Healthcare IoT** applications like remote patient monitoring and AI-driven diagnostics rely on fast data transmission for accurate and timely responses.

4. Energy Efficiency for IoT Devices

- 5G's advanced power-saving features (such as **NB-IoT and LTE-M**) extend the battery life of IoT devices, which is crucial for **low-power applications** like environmental sensors and smart meters.
- **Example: IoT-enabled sensors in agriculture** can operate for years without requiring frequent battery replacements.

1.4.3 Key IoT Applications by 5G

Smart Cities

- **Traffic management:** Real-time traffic monitoring and smart traffic lights reduce congestion.
- **Public safety:** AI-driven surveillance cameras enhance security and emergency response.
- **Smart grids:** IoT-enabled energy grids optimize power distribution and reduce outages.

Healthcare & Remote Monitoring

- **5G-enabled wearable devices** track patient health in real time.
- **Remote surgeries:** Doctors can perform robotic-assisted surgeries from anywhere with **ultra-low latency 5G networks.**

Industrial IoT (IIoT) & Smart Manufacturing

- **Automated factories** use 5G for **robotic arms, AI-driven quality checks, and predictive maintenance.**
- **Supply chain tracking:** IoT sensors monitor the location and condition of goods in transit.

Autonomous Vehicles & Transportation

- **Self-driving cars** rely on 5G for **instant vehicle-to-vehicle (V2V) and vehicle-to-infrastructure (V2I) communication.**
- **Smart traffic control systems** reduce congestion and enhance road safety.
- Precision Agriculture
- **IoT-powered drones and sensors** monitor soil conditions, water levels, and crop health.
- **5G connectivity** allows farmers to receive real-time updates and automate irrigation and fertilization.

1.4.4 Challenges and Future of 5G-Enabled IoT

Challenges

- **High Infrastructure Costs:** Deploying 5G networks and IoT devices requires significant investment.
- **Security & Privacy Risks:** More connected devices mean an increased risk of cyberattacks and data breaches.
- **Network Coverage Issues:** Rural and remote areas may face delays in 5G deployment.

The Future of 5G & IoT

- **6G & AI Integration:** Future networks will offer even faster speeds and AI-powered automation.
- **Edge Computing & IoT Growth:** 5G will enable **real-time edge computing**, reducing data processing delays.
- **Widespread IoT Adoption:** From homes to industries, IoT will become an integral part of daily life, powered by seamless 5G connectivity.

The integration of **5G and IoT** marks the beginning of a new digital era, where **smart, connected devices** will enhance efficiency, safety, and convenience across industries. With **ultra-low latency, high-speed data transfer, and massive connectivity**, 5G is the backbone that will enable IoT to reach its full potential. As both technologies continue to evolve, they will revolutionize **smart cities, healthcare, transportation, and industrial automation**, shaping a future driven by intelligent connectivity.

CASE STUDY ON MOBILE COMMUNICATION

Case Study

The Evolution and Impact of Mobile Communication

Introduction

Mobile communication has revolutionized the way people interact, work, and access information. From the first mobile phone call in 1973 to today's 5G-enabled smartphones, the technology has evolved significantly. This case study explores the growth of mobile communication, its impact on industries, and future trends.

Background

The Evolution of Mobile Communication

1G to 5G Technology Evolution

- **1G (1980s):** First-generation mobile networks introduced analog voice calls.
- **2G (1990s):** Digital networks enabled SMS and basic data services.
- **3G (2000s):** Allowed mobile internet, video calls, and app-based services.
- **4G (2010s):** High-speed data, video streaming, and mobile broadband.
- **5G (2020s and beyond):** Ultra-fast speeds, low latency, and IoT connectivity.

Case Example

Mobile Communication in Business (The Rise of Mobile Banking in Africa)

Problem

In many African countries, traditional banking infrastructure was limited, making financial transactions difficult, especially in rural areas.

Solution

The introduction of **mobile banking** services like **M-Pesa (Kenya)** allowed people to send, receive, and store money using mobile phones.

Results

- Over **50 million users** adopted M-Pesa across multiple countries.
- Increased financial inclusion, with millions gaining access to banking services.
- Boosted economic activities, allowing small businesses to thrive.

Impact of Mobile Communication on Society

1. Social Impact

- **Increased Connectivity:** Mobile phones connect people globally.
- **Emergency Services:** Mobile networks help in disaster management.
- **Education:** Mobile learning apps provide access to knowledge.

2. Business Impact

- **E-commerce Growth:** Businesses use mobile apps for sales and marketing.
- **Remote Work:** Mobile communication supports remote jobs and collaboration.
- **Mobile Payments:** Digital wallets (PayPal, Google Pay) revolutionized transactions.

3. Technological Impact

- **Smartphone Innovation:** AI, augmented reality (AR), and virtual assistants.
- **Internet of Things (IoT):** Smart homes and connected devices use mobile networks.
- **5G & Beyond:** Future advancements will enable real-time applications like autonomous cars.

Challenges in Mobile Communication

- **Cybersecurity Threats:** Mobile hacking and data breaches are rising.
- **Digital Divide:** Rural areas still lack mobile network access.
- **Health Concerns:** Overuse of mobile devices leads to health issues like digital addiction.

Future of Mobile Communication

- **6G Networks:** Expected to offer speeds of **100 Gbps** and ultra-low latency.
- **AI-powered Communication:** Smart AI assistants will enhance user experience.
- **Satellite Internet Integration:** Companies like Starlink aim to bring global mobile coverage.

Mobile communication has transformed how we live and work. While it brings immense benefits, challenges like cybersecurity and accessibility must be addressed. Future advancements will continue shaping the digital world.

TEACHERS KNOW MORE

- Broadband refers to **high-speed internet access** that is always on and faster than traditional dial-up.
- It has transformed **education, business, healthcare, and entertainment.**

The Rise of Broadband (2000s)

- Introduction of **DSL, Cable, and Fiber Optic Internet** allowed faster speeds.
- Enabled **online education, video streaming, and cloud storage.**
- Schools started using broadband for **digital learning and research.**

Mobile Broadband & Wireless Internet (2010s)

- **3G & 4G Networks** made the internet accessible on mobile devices.
- Introduction of **Wi-Fi networks** boosted online learning and work.
- **E-learning platforms (Google Classroom, Zoom, YouTube)** became essential in education.

2 5G: A Network of Opporunity

Outcome

- **5G Architecture**: Network components, radio access technology (NR), and core network design.
- **Spectrum and Frequency Bands**: Low-band, mid-band, and high-band (mm Wave) utilization.
- **Performance Requirements**: Speed, latency, and connection density standards.
- **Key Enabling Technologies**: Massive MIMO, beamforming, edge computing, and network slicing.
- **Security and Privacy Considerations**: Protection against cyber threats and data vulnerabilities.

The world is on the brink of a technological revolution, one that promises to reshape industries, economies, and everyday life. At the heart of this transformation is **5G**, the fifth generation of wireless technology. More than just an upgrade to faster internet speeds, 5G represents a fundamental shift in how we connect, communicate, and innovate. For decades, each new generation of mobile networks has unlocked new possibilities. **1G** introduced mobile voice calls, **2G** brought text messaging, **3G** enabled mobile internet, and **4G LTE** revolutionized streaming, gaming, and app-based businesses. Now, 5G is set to take things even further—with ultra-fast speeds, near-zero latency, and the capacity to connect billions of devices simultaneously.

The implications of this breakthrough extend beyond smartphones. **Healthcare**, **transportation**, **manufacturing**, **education**, and even **entertainment** are being reshaped by 5G's potential. Imagine remote surgeries performed with robotic precision, self-driving cars communicating in real-time to avoid accidents, and smart cities optimizing energy use and reducing traffic congestion. These aren't futuristic dreams—they're fast becoming reality. However, as with any technological leap, challenges remain. Infrastructure deployment, security concerns, and the digital divide are just some of the hurdles that need to be addressed. Yet, the opportunities far outweigh the obstacles. Businesses, governments, and individuals must prepare to harness the full potential of 5G to stay ahead in a rapidly evolving digital landscape. **5G is more than just a network—it's a catalyst for innovation and economic growth**. From its technological foundations to its real-world applications and future possibilities, we will dive into what makes 5G such a game-changer. Whether you're a tech enthusiast, business leader, or simply curious about what's next, this journey into the world of 5G will reveal how this next-generation network is unlocking new opportunities for all.

2.1 5G DESIGN SPECIFICATION

The evolution of wireless communication has led to a significant transformation in the way we connect, compute, and interact. **5G (Fifth-Generation Wireless Technology)** is designed to be more than just an incremental upgrade—it is a complete reimagining of network architecture, performance, and capabilities. Unlike its predecessors, 5G is engineered to support a vast array of applications, from ultra-fast mobile broadband to mission-critical communications and massive IoT (Internet of Things) connectivity.

This document provides an in-depth exploration of the **design specifications** that define 5G technology. It outlines the fundamental principles, key requirements, and architectural innovations that set 5G apart from previous generations. By understanding these design specifications, stakeholders—including network operators, engineers, policymakers, and businesses—can effectively deploy and optimize 5G networks to maximize their potential.

2.1.1 Key Objectives of 5G Design

The development of 5G networks is guided by several fundamental objectives:

1. **Enhanced Data Speeds:** 5G aims to deliver speeds of up to **10 Gbps**, significantly outpacing 4G LTE.
2. **Ultra-Low Latency:** With latencies as low as **1 millisecond**, 5G enables real-time communication critical for applications such as autonomous driving and remote surgeries.
3. **Massive Connectivity:** 5G is designed to support **over a million devices per square kilometer**, enabling the growth of smart cities and industrial IoT.
4. **Energy Efficiency:** Advanced power-saving mechanisms ensure optimal energy consumption for both devices and network infrastructure.
5. **Network Slicing:** A virtualized architecture that allows customized network experiences for different industries and applications.
6. **Security and Reliability:** Enhanced encryption, authentication, and threat detection mechanisms to ensure a **secure and resilient** network.

This design specification covers the following core aspects of 5G technology:

- **5G Architecture**: Network components, radio access technology (NR), and core network design.
- **Spectrum and Frequency Bands**: Low-band, mid-band, and high-band (mm Wave) utilization.
- **Performance Requirements**: Speed, latency, and connection density standards.
- **Key Enabling Technologies**: Massive MIMO, beamforming, edge computing, and network slicing.
- **Security and Privacy Considerations**: Protection against cyber threats and data vulnerabilities.

As the global rollout of 5G continues, understanding these design principles is crucial for ensuring a seamless, efficient, and secure transition to next-generation networks. This document serves as a comprehensive guide to **the technical foundation and strategic vision of 5G**, equipping readers with the knowledge needed to navigate the complexities of this revolutionary technology.

2.2 FREQUENCY BANDS IN 5G

5G technology operates across a wide range of frequency bands, categorized primarily into **low-band, mid-band, and high-band (millimetre-wave or mmWave)** spectrums. Each of these bands has unique characteristics that define their performance in terms of **coverage, speed, latency, and capacity**. The selection and deployment of these frequency bands vary based on regional regulations, network requirements, and specific use cases.

> **Interesting Fact**
>
> Your Microwave Uses a Similar Frequency as Wi-Fi. Most home microwaves operate at 2.45 GHz, close to the 2.4 GHz Wi-Fi band. That's why interference can happen when both are running at the same time.

2.2.1 Low-Band (Sub-1 GHz) Spectrum

Frequency Range: Below **1 GHz** (e.g., 600 MHz, 700 MHz, 800 MHz, 900 MHz)

Characteristics

- **Widest coverage area:** Low-band frequencies can travel long distances, making them ideal for providing broad coverage in **rural and suburban areas**.
- **Strong penetration through obstacles:** They can **easily penetrate walls and buildings**, ensuring reliable indoor connectivity.
- **Lower data speeds compared to higher bands:** Peak speeds typically range between **50 Mbps to 300 Mbps**, which is **better than 4G but significantly slower** than mid-band or mmWave.
- **Ideal for basic 5G applications** like IoT connectivity, voice services, and mobile broadband in remote areas.

Use Cases

- Nationwide 5G coverage in rural areas
- IoT (Internet of Things) applications
- Basic mobile broadband connectivity

2.2.2 Mid-Band (1 GHz - 7 GHz) Spectrum

Frequency Range: 1 GHz to 7 GHz (e.g., 2.5 GHz, 3.5 GHz, 4.9 GHz, C-band 3.7-4.2 GHz)

Characteristics

- **Balanced coverage and speed:** Mid-band provides a compromise between **range and capacity**, making it the **most widely used** 5G band worldwide.
- **Faster speeds (300 Mbps - 1 Gbps):** Mid-band 5G offers significantly higher data rates than low-band, supporting most high-speed applications.
- **Moderate penetration capabilities:** While mid-band signals can penetrate buildings, they may not be as effective as low-band frequencies.
- **Best suited for urban and suburban deployments**, where a balance between speed and coverage is required.

Use Cases

- Enhanced mobile broadband (eMBB) for urban and suburban users
- Smart cities and connected vehicles
- Enterprise applications, including **5G private networks**

2.2.3 High-Band (Millimeter-Wave or mmWave, 24 GHz - 100 GHz) Spectrum

Frequency Range: 24 GHz to 100 GHz (e.g., 26 GHz, 28 GHz, 39 GHz, 60 GHz)

Characteristics

- **Extremely high data speeds (1 Gbps - 10 Gbps):** Millimeter-wave frequencies enable **fiber-like wireless speeds**, essential for data-heavy applications.
- **Ultra-low latency (<1 ms):** Enables **real-time applications** such as remote surgery, autonomous vehicles, and cloud gaming.
- **Limited coverage range:** High-band frequencies have a **short transmission range** (typically a few hundred meters) and are **easily blocked by walls, trees, and weather conditions.**
- **Requires dense network infrastructure:** To overcome the limited range, **small cells** and advanced beamforming techniques are deployed.

Use Cases

- High-speed mobile broadband in **dense urban areas**
- **Fixed Wireless Access (FWA)** for high-speed home broadband
- **Smart stadiums, airports, and shopping malls**
- **Augmented Reality (AR), Virtual Reality (VR), and cloud gaming**
- **Comparison of 5G Frequency Bands**

Spectrum Band	Frequency Range	Cove-rage	Speed	Penetra-tion	Latency	Use Cases
Low-Band	Sub-1 GHz	High	Low (50-300 Mbps)	Strong	Higher (~10 ms)	Rural coverage, IoT, voice services
Mid-Band	1 GHz - 7 GHz	Medium	Medium (300 Mbps - 1 Gbps)	Moderate	Low (~5 ms)	Urban/sub-urban 5G, smart cities, enterprise applications
High-Band (mmWave)	24 GHz - 100 GHz	Low	High (1-10 Gbps)	Weak	Ultra-low (<1 ms)	Cloud gam-ing, AR/VR, autonomous vehicles, FWA

2.2.4 Global 5G Spectrum Allocations

Regulatory bodies worldwide have assigned specific frequency bands for 5G, with variations in different regions:

- **United States (FCC):** Uses low-band (600 MHz), mid-band (C-band 3.7-3.98 GHz), and mmWave (28 GHz, 39 GHz).
- **Europe (ETSI):** Focuses on 700 MHz (low-band), 3.4-3.8 GHz (mid-band), and 26 GHz (mmWave).
- **China:** Uses 2.6 GHz, 3.5 GHz, and 4.9 GHz mid-band frequencies, along with mmWave bands.
- **India (TRAI):** Allocates 700 MHz (low-band), 3.3-3.67 GHz (mid-band), and trials mmWave bands like 26 GHz.

Each country optimizes its spectrum usage based on **available bandwidth, regulatory policies, and network operator strategies.**

2.2.5 Future of 5G Spectrum and Beyond

- **6G Development:** Future wireless networks will push into even higher frequencies (**100 GHz - 1 THz**) for ultra-high-speed communication.
- **Dynamic Spectrum Sharing (DSS):** Enables **4G and 5G to coexist** in the same frequency bands, improving deployment efficiency.
- **Expanded mmWave and Satellite Integration:** 5G is expected to integrate with **Low Earth Orbit (LEO) satellites**, expanding coverage to remote areas.

> mmWave Can Be Blocked by Everyday Objects: High-frequency mmWave signals (24 GHz+) struggle to penetrate walls, trees, and even rain. That's why small cell towers are needed every few hundred meters for proper coverage.
>
> *Interesting Fact*

As 5G adoption accelerates, **effective spectrum management** will be crucial in ensuring **optimal performance, reliability, and connectivity** across various industries. The success of 5G depends on **strategic frequency band utilization**, balancing **coverage, speed, and network capacity**. Low-band ensures wide coverage, mid-band delivers a strong mix of speed and range, while high-band mmWave unlocks ultra-fast data rates for next-generation applications. Understanding these **frequency bands** allows businesses, telecom operators, and policymakers to deploy **optimized 5G networks** that meet the demands of the modern digital world.

2.3 BEAMFORMING IN 5G: A DETAILED EXPLANATION

Beamforming is an advanced **signal processing** technique used in 5G wireless networks to improve signal quality, coverage, and data rates. It allows a base station to **dynamically direct radio signals** toward specific users or devices rather than broadcasting them in all directions. This targeted approach **enhances efficiency, reduces interference, and improves overall network performance**.

In traditional cellular networks (e.g., 4G LTE), antennas transmit signals in all directions, leading to **signal loss and interference**. In contrast, 5G networks use **Massive MIMO (Multiple Input Multiple Output) antennas** combined with beamforming to focus energy where it's needed most.

2.3.1 Beamforming Working

Beamforming relies on **multiple antennas** at the base station, working together to shape and steer signals. By adjusting the **phase and amplitude** of transmitted signals, the base station creates **constructive interference** in the desired direction and **destructive interference** in others, effectively forming a signal "beam."

2.3.2 Steps in Beamforming

1. **User Device Detection:** The base station detects the location of the user device and determines the best path for signal transmission.
2. **Phase & Amplitude Adjustment:** Signals from multiple antennas are adjusted to align in a way that strengthens the signal toward the user.
3. **Beam Steering:** The signal beam is directed toward the user dynamically, adapting to their movement and changing network conditions.

This precise control enables **better signal strength, reduced interference, and higher data speeds** compared to traditional broadcasting.

2.3.3 Types of Beamforming in 5G

1. Analog Beamforming

- Uses a single **RF chain** to control multiple antennas.
- **All antennas transmit the same signal** with phase adjustments to focus energy in a specific direction.
- Efficient in **mmWave (high-band) 5G** for directional signal transmission.
- **Limitation:** Cannot support multiple beams simultaneously.

2. Digital Beamforming

- Uses separate **RF chains** for each antenna element, allowing independent control.
- Supports **multiple beams for multiple users simultaneously** (Massive MIMO).
- Enables **precise interference reduction** and improved spectral efficiency.
- More complex but **ideal for mid-band 5G networks**.

3. Hybrid Beamforming

- A combination of **analog and digital beamforming** to balance complexity and efficiency.
- Used in **both mid-band and mmWave 5G** to optimize performance.
- Provides multiple beams while reducing hardware complexity and energy consumption.

2.3.4 Benefits of Beamforming in 5G

1. **Higher Data Speeds:** Focused signals ensure better **signal-to-noise ratio (SNR)**, leading to **faster data transmission**.
2. **Extended Coverage:** Beamforming improves network reach, especially in **mmWave** deployments, where signals are typically weaker.
3. **Reduced Interference:** Directing signals toward users **minimizes interference** from other devices and networks.

4. **Improved Energy Efficiency:** Concentrating signal power reduces **unnecessary energy consumption**, making networks more sustainable.
5. **Better User Experience:** Stronger and more reliable connections, especially in **dense urban environments**.

2.3.5 Challenges of Beamforming

- **Increased Complexity:** Requires sophisticated algorithms and real-time adjustments.
- **High Processing Power:** Beamforming relies on advanced computing and AI-driven optimizations.
- **Deployment Cost:** Massive MIMO and beamforming hardware can be **expensive to implement**.
- **Obstruction Sensitivity:** In mmWave frequencies, signals can still be blocked by **buildings, trees, and other objects**.

2.3.6 Real-World Applications of Beamforming in 5G

✓ **Urban 5G Networks:** Beamforming enhances coverage and speeds in **high-density areas** (e.g., smart cities).

✓ **Autonomous Vehicles:** Ensures **low-latency communication** for self-driving cars.

✓ **Fixed Wireless Access (FWA):** Delivers high-speed broadband to homes and businesses.

✓ **Augmented & Virtual Reality (AR/VR):** Provides stable, high-speed connections for immersive experiences.

Beamforming is a **core technology in 5G** that enhances **signal quality, efficiency, and user experience**. By **focusing signals dynamically**, 5G networks achieve **higher speeds, better coverage, and reduced interference**, making them **more reliable and efficient** than previous wireless generations.

2.4 DIRECTIONALITY IN 5G

Directionality in 5G refers to the ability of **wireless signals to be transmitted and received in a focused manner**, rather than being broadcast in all directions. Unlike previous generations of wireless networks (such as 4G LTE), where signals are **omnidirectional** (spread equally in all directions), 5G uses **directional signal transmission** to improve **efficiency, speed, and reliability**. This directionality is achieved using **beamforming** and **Massive MIMO (Multiple Input Multiple Output)** technologies, which enable the network to direct signals toward specific users, devices, or areas, rather than wasting energy in unnecessary directions.

2.4.1 Directionality Working in 5G

1. Beamforming for Focused Transmission

- In **traditional wireless networks**, signals are broadcasted in all directions, leading to **signal loss and interference**.
- **5G uses beamforming** to concentrate signals toward a **specific user or device**, ensuring **stronger connectivity and higher efficiency**.

- The base station **adjusts the phase and amplitude of signals** from multiple antennas to create a **directional beam** toward the intended receiver.

2. Massive MIMO for Multiple Beams

- **Massive MIMO** uses a large number of antennas at the base station to **create multiple focused beams.**
- Instead of a single omnidirectional signal, **multiple users can receive dedicated directional signals simultaneously**.
- This increases **network capacity, data speeds, and reduces interference** in high-density areas.

3. Millimeter-Wave (mmWave) Directionality

- **High-frequency mmWave signals (24 GHz - 100 GHz) naturally have more directionality** due to their shorter wavelengths.
- These signals can be **easily focused into narrow beams**, allowing 5G networks to **transmit ultra-high-speed data** efficiently.
- However, mmWave signals are **more sensitive to obstacles**, requiring techniques like **beam tracking and beam switching** to maintain stable connections.

2.4.2 Benefits of Directionality in 5G

✓ **Higher Data Speeds:** Directing signals toward users ensures **stronger connections and faster transmission rates** (1 Gbps: 10 Gbps).

✓ **Reduced Interference:** Focused beams **avoid unnecessary signal overlap**, improving network stability.

✓ **Improved Coverage & Capacity:** Directionality enables **better connectivity in crowded environments** (e.g., stadiums, smart cities).

✓ **Energy Efficiency:** Transmitting signals only where needed **reduces power consumption** for both base stations and devices.

✓ **Better Performance in Urban Areas:** Directional transmission helps **overcome signal blockage by buildings** and other obstacles.

2.4.3 Challenges of Directionality in 5G

- **Requires Advanced Antennas & Processing:** Beamforming and Massive MIMO need **highly complex algorithms and real-time calculations.**
- **Sensitivity to Obstacles:** High-frequency directional signals (e.g., mmWave) can be **blocked by walls, trees, and even rain**, requiring additional solutions like **beam tracking and relay stations.**
- **Higher Deployment Costs:** Implementing **directional antennas and smart beamforming** requires **significant investment** in infrastructure.

2.4.4 Real-World Applications of 5G Directionality

- **Smart Cities:** Directing signals efficiently ensures **seamless connectivity for IoT devices, cameras, and sensors.**
- **Autonomous Vehicles:** Vehicles use **directional 5G signals** for real-time communication and **low-latency navigation.**

- **Cloud Gaming & AR/VR:** Directionality enables **lag-free, high-speed streaming for immersive experiences.**
- **Fixed Wireless Access (FWA):** 5G home broadband benefits from **highly directional mmWave signals** for **fiber-like speeds.**

Directionality is a key feature of 5G that enables **faster speeds, lower latency, and better network efficiency.** By focusing signals in the required direction, 5G networks overcome many limitations of traditional broadcasting methods, making them ideal for **high-speed, high-density, and mission-critical applications.**

Your Phone Uses Directionality Without You Knowing: Modern smartphones automatically adjust their antenna direction for the strongest signal, depending on how you hold or move your device.

Interesting Fact

2.5 ADVANTAGES OF 5G DESIGN SPECIFICATION

5G is designed to deliver **high-speed, low-latency, and highly reliable** communication, supporting a wide range of applications across industries. The 5G design specification introduces **advanced technologies** such as **Massive MIMO, beamforming, network slicing, and millimeter-wave (mmWave) communication**, significantly improving network performance compared to previous generations.

2.5.1 Key Advantages of 5G Design Specification

1. Ultra-Fast Speeds

- 5G networks provide speeds up to **10 Gbps**, which is **100 times faster** than 4G LTE.
- High-speed data transmission enables **seamless streaming, cloud gaming, AR/VR applications, and real-time data sharing.**
- Faster downloads and uploads reduce **buffering and lag**, improving the overall user experience.

2. Ultra-Low Latency

- 5G reduces latency to **as low as 1 millisecond (ms)**, compared to **30-50 ms in 4G LTE.**
- Essential for **real-time applications** such as **autonomous vehicles, remote surgeries, and industrial automation.**
- Enables **instantaneous communication** for mission-critical operations.

3. Higher Network Capacity

- Uses **Massive MIMO (Multiple Input Multiple Output)** technology, allowing **more simultaneous connections.**
- Supports up to **1 million devices per square kilometer**, ideal for **IoT (Internet of Things) and smart city deployments.**
- Reduces congestion, ensuring smooth connectivity even in crowded areas.

4. Enhanced Coverage and Reliability

- 5G operates across multiple **frequency bands (low, mid, and high-band/mmWave)**, providing **flexible coverage options.**
- **Beamforming technology** directs signals efficiently, reducing interference and improving network reliability.
- Ensures **consistent connectivity in urban, suburban, and rural areas.**

5. Improved Energy Efficiency

- **Optimized network resource allocation** minimizes power consumption.
- Devices can operate in **low-power modes**, extending battery life for **IoT devices and mobile users.**
- Reduces carbon footprint, making 5G a **more sustainable** wireless technology.

6. Support for Advanced Applications

5G enables cutting-edge applications such as: Autonomous vehicles (real-time vehicle-to-vehicle communication), Remote healthcare (telemedicine, robotic surgeries), Industrial automation (smart factories, predictive maintenance), Smart cities (IoT-connected infrastructure, traffic management), AR/VR and cloud gaming (immersive experiences without lag)

7. Network Slicing for Customization

- Allows operators to **create multiple virtual networks** (network slices) on a **single physical infrastructure.**
- Each slice can be **customized for different industries** (e.g., low-latency for healthcare, high-speed for gaming, massive connectivity for IoT).
- Ensures **better resource allocation and service quality** for different use cases.

8. Seamless Integration with Existing Technologies

- **Dynamic Spectrum Sharing (DSS)** allows 5G to coexist with **4G LTE**, enabling a **smooth transition** for operators and users.
- **Backward compatibility** ensures that older devices can still connect to networks during the 5G rollout.
- 5G can work alongside **Wi-Fi 6, AI**, and **cloud computing** to enhance network capabilities.

The **5G design specification** brings significant improvements in **speed, capacity, latency, and efficiency**, making it a **transformative technology** for businesses, industries, and consumers. With its ability to support **next-generation applications**, 5G is set to revolutionize communication, automation, and digital experiences across the globe.

CASE STUDY: BEAMFORMING IN 5G NETWORKS

Overview

Beamforming is a technique used in wireless communication to direct radio waves towards a specific user or device rather than broadcasting the signal in all directions. It leverages multiple antennas at the transmitter (base station) and/or receiver (mobile device) to focus the signal, resulting in better performance, reduced interference, and higher data rates. In

5G, beamforming plays a crucial role in achieving high data throughput and low latency by improving spectrum efficiency and optimizing signal coverage. This case study will explore **beamforming** in the context of a **5G deployment** by a telecommunications company in an urban environment.

URBAN DEPLOYMENT BY TELCOX

Background

TelcoX is a global telecommunications company that recently deployed 5G infrastructure in a densely populated urban area. Their goal was to deliver ultra-fast 5G services with reduced latency, higher reliability, and massive connectivity for IoT devices. Given the challenges posed by urban environments, including interference from buildings, high user density, and diverse use cases (e.g., video streaming, gaming, and IoT), the company adopted beamforming as a core component of its 5G network design.

Challenges

1. **High User Density**: In dense urban areas, users are often clustered together, which leads to significant signal interference. Conventional omnidirectional antennas struggle to manage traffic in such environments.
2. **Urban Interference**: The presence of buildings and other obstacles can result in multipath fading, where signals take multiple paths to reach the receiver. This causes signal degradation.
3. **Limited Spectrum**: The 5G spectrum is limited, and without efficient use, it can lead to congestion, reducing overall network performance.
4. **Service Demand**: The demand for high data rates for applications like AR/VR, video streaming, and connected devices (IoT) is rapidly increasing.

Solution

TelcoX implemented **Massive MIMO (Multiple Input, Multiple Output)** technology with beamforming capabilities at its 5G base stations to address these challenges. The deployment strategy included:

1. **Massive MIMO Antennas**: They used base stations equipped with arrays of 64 to 128 antennas, enabling the transmission of multiple data streams simultaneously. These antennas could adapt their beamforming directions dynamically based on user location and network conditions.
2. **Dynamic Beamforming**: The system continuously adjusted the direction and shape of the beam to target specific users or devices. This was done using real-time data on user location, signal strength, and interference levels.
3. **High-Frequency Bands (mmWave)**: TelcoX focused on mmWave frequencies for high data throughput. While mmWave is prone to higher attenuation (especially due to physical obstructions like buildings), beamforming helped focus signals on users, overcoming some of the limitations of mmWave.
4. **Beam Tracking**: In a fast-moving environment (e.g., with mobile users), beamforming algorithms tracked the users' movement, adjusting beams in real-time to ensure consistent connectivity without requiring users to stay in fixed positions.

Implementation

- **Base Stations**: TelcoX upgraded its base stations with advanced 5G Massive MIMO antennas capable of performing beamforming with a large number of antennas (up to 128).
- **User Equipment**: To fully take advantage of beamforming, users needed compatible devices (smartphones, routers) with beamforming support. TelcoX collaborated with device manufacturers to ensure that its customers had access to compatible devices.
- **Software and Algorithms**: Advanced software and AI algorithms were implemented to optimize beamforming in real-time, dynamically adapting beam directions, user prioritization, and network resources based on traffic demands.

Results

1. **Enhanced Coverage and Capacity**: Beamforming significantly improved coverage, especially in urban areas where traditional omnidirectional antennas were ineffective. The signals were more focused, reducing interference and improving signal quality, even in heavily congested areas.
2. **Improved Data Throughput**: The focus on specific users or devices allowed TelcoX to achieve high data rates, with some users experiencing speeds exceeding 1 Gbps, particularly in mmWave bands.
3. **Reduced Latency**: Beamforming minimized signal delays by focusing the radio waves in a direct line of sight to users, reducing latency to under 5 ms for many use cases.
4. **Better Spectrum Utilization**: By using beamforming, TelcoX was able to make efficient use of the available spectrum, increasing capacity without the need for additional spectrum allocations.
5. **Improved User Experience**: TelcoX observed a substantial improvement in the quality of service for users, with fewer dropped calls, improved video streaming quality, and lower latency for interactive applications like gaming.

Points to Remember

- **Dynamic Optimization**: Continuous real-time optimization of beamforming is crucial for maintaining high performance, especially in urban environments where users' locations and network conditions are constantly changing.
- **Interoperability**: The success of beamforming in the 5G network was dependent on ensuring that both base stations and user devices were compatible and could communicate effectively with one another.
- **Cost vs. Benefit**: While the initial costs of deploying massive MIMO antennas and the necessary infrastructure were high, the long-term benefits in terms of network efficiency, user experience, and scalability justified the investment.

Beamforming technology played a pivotal role in TelcoX's 5G network deployment in urban areas. By focusing radio signals directly to users, the company was able to mitigate interference, optimize spectrum usage, and deliver high-speed, low-latency services to a large number of connected devices. This case study demonstrates how advanced techniques like beamforming can address the challenges posed by urban environments in the next-generation wireless communication systems.

REAL-TIME APPLICATION OF DIRECTIONALITY IN 5G: SMART MANUFACTURING (INDUSTRIAL IOT)

One of the key features of 5G networks is **directionality**, which is made possible by technologies like **beamforming** and **Massive MIMO**. Directionality refers to the ability of a network to focus radio signals in specific directions to enhance performance, improve signal quality, and reduce interference. This capability plays a crucial role in real-time applications that demand high reliability and low latency, such as **Smart Manufacturing** in industrial IoT environments.

Application: Smart Manufacturing in Industrial IoT (IIoT)

Overview

Smart manufacturing involves using connected devices, sensors, and automation systems to improve production processes, monitor equipment health, and enable real-time decision-making. 5G's ability to provide high-speed connectivity with low latency and efficient directionality is critical for ensuring seamless communication between machines, workers, and control systems.

Role of Directionality in Smart Manufacturing

In this context, **directionality** in 5G, particularly through beamforming and Massive MIMO technology, provides several benefits that enhance the performance and efficiency of the manufacturing process.

Key Aspects of Directionality in 5G for Smart Manufacturing

1. Real-Time Machine Monitoring

- **Use Case**: Industrial machines and robots are equipped with IoT sensors that constantly transmit data to a central control system. This data includes information such as temperature, pressure, vibration levels, and operating speeds.
- **How Directionality Helps**: Beamforming directs signals towards the machines, allowing for reliable, real-time data transmission without interference from other machines or environmental factors. This ensures that critical data, such as equipment health metrics, are transmitted with minimal delay and maximum accuracy.
- **Impact**: With improved signal directionality, the system can detect anomalies or potential failures in machines much faster, leading to more timely maintenance and less downtime.

2. Autonomous Mobile Robots (AMRs) and Drones

- **Use Case**: In smart factories, **Autonomous Mobile Robots** (**AMRs**) and drones are used for material transport, inventory management, and inspection tasks. These robots require constant communication with central systems to navigate the factory floor, avoid obstacles, and ensure task completion.
- **How Directionality Helps**: 5G's beamforming allows for focused, high-speed communication between the central control system and mobile robots or drones. The ability to maintain strong, uninterrupted signals improves the accuracy of navigation, real-time updates, and collision avoidance.

- **Impact**: Directional signals ensure seamless communication, reducing the risk of communication loss in dynamic environments and enabling robots to operate autonomously with high precision.

3. Enhanced Augmented Reality (AR) for Maintenance and Training

- **Use Case**: Technicians in the factory can use **augmented reality (AR)** devices to visualize equipment, receive step-by-step repair instructions, or perform remote troubleshooting with the help of experts.
- **How Directionality Helps**: Beamforming can direct signals to AR headsets worn by technicians, providing high-quality, low-latency video feeds from remote experts or visualizing sensor data without interference. This ensures that AR applications work smoothly in real-time, even in areas with high traffic or potential signal interference.
- **Impact**: Directionality enhances the AR experience by ensuring clear and real-time communication, improving maintenance accuracy and reducing operational costs due to faster repairs.

4. Real-Time Quality Control

- **Use Case**: In production lines, **quality control systems** use cameras, sensors, and machines to inspect products for defects and ensure they meet the required standards.
- **How Directionality Helps**: With 5G's ability to direct signals, cameras and sensors transmitting data to the quality control system can maintain high-speed, low-latency communication, even in environments with heavy machinery or high user density. The system can quickly analyze the product quality and transmit the results to control systems in real-time.
- **Impact**: Directionality reduces the chances of signal interference, allowing for real-time product inspection and ensuring high-quality manufacturing without delays or errors.

5. Edge Computing Integration

- **Use Case**: In some factories, edge computing devices are deployed to process data locally before sending it to the cloud. This minimizes latency and enhances real-time decision-making.
- **How Directionality Helps**: Beamforming ensures that edge devices in the factory receive strong and stable connections, even in areas with high interference or multiple devices communicating at once. This allows edge devices to process data quickly and make instantaneous decisions based on local inputs, without waiting for cloud-based processing.
- **Impact**: With precise directional signals, the factory can perform real-time analytics at the edge, enabling faster responses to changing production conditions, such as adjusting machine parameters or optimizing workflows.

Benefits of Directionality in Smart Manufacturing with 5G

- **Improved Network Efficiency**: Directional beams reduce interference and increase the overall network efficiency, ensuring that communication between machines, sensors, and control systems is not only fast but also reliable.

- **Reduced Latency**: With focused, high-speed connections, 5G minimizes delays in communication, ensuring that time-sensitive operations like autonomous navigation or real-time maintenance can be done efficiently without disruption.
- **Increased System Reliability**: Directionality ensures that signal quality is maintained even in environments with a high concentration of devices. This reduces the risk of communication dropouts, ensuring more consistent system performance.
- **Scalability**: As factories add more IoT devices, robots, and machines, the network can scale efficiently by leveraging the ability to focus signals where they are needed, without overloading the system.
- **Support for Mission-Critical Applications**: The high reliability, low latency, and focused communication enabled by directionality in 5G make it ideal for mission-critical applications such as remote surgery, automated machinery, and precision manufacturing processes.

The real-time application of directionality in 5G within **Smart Manufacturing** demonstrates how crucial technologies like beamforming and Massive MIMO can optimize industrial operations. By providing focused, low-latency, and high-speed communication, 5G enhances the performance, reliability, and efficiency of IoT systems in manufacturing. This creates opportunities for higher productivity, reduced operational costs, and improved product quality—all essential for maintaining competitive advantage in today's rapidly evolving industrial landscape.

TEACHERS KNOW MORE

- **High Throughput and Low LatencyDesign goal:** 5G networks are designed to provide ultra-high throughput (up to 100 Gbps) and ultra-low latency (less than 1 millisecond) to support applications requiring massive data transfer and real-time communications, such as augmented reality (AR), virtual reality (VR), and autonomous vehicles.
- **Network Slicing:** Flexibility in resource allocation: 5G supports network slicing, which allows the creation of multiple virtual networks tailored to the specific needs of different applications. This enables more efficient use of resources, improved quality of service (QoS), and enhanced user experience for various services (e.g., IoT, broadband, mission-critical communications).
- **Massive Device Connectivity (IoT):** Scalability: 5G includes support for connecting a massive number of devices (up to 1 million devices per square kilometre). This feature is critical for enabling the Internet of Things (IoT) and the growing number of connected devices in smart cities, industrial automation, and agriculture.
- **Advanced Radio Technologies:** MIMO and mmWave: 5G incorporates advanced radio technologies like **Massive MIMO** (Multiple Input, Multiple Output) and **millimeter-wave (mmWave)** frequencies. Massive MIMO allows for more efficient use of spectrum by using a large number of antennas, while mmWave provides high-speed data transfer by utilizing higher frequency bands (24 GHz and above).
- **Energy Efficiency:** Sustainability. 5G networks are designed to be energy-efficient, optimizing power usage across base stations, devices, and network components. This is crucial for both reducing operational costs for telecom providers and supporting global sustainability goals by minimizing the carbon footprint of the network.

Intentionally left blank!

3 IoT Applications

3.1 LOCALIZATION

Localization can refer to the process of identifying the geographic position of an object, person, or device and tracking the position while the object is in motion using various technologies such as GPS, Wi-Fi, Bluetooth, 5G Radio waves and other sensors. There are 2 types of localization.

- **Geographical Positioning System (GPS)**: This involves determining the precise location of a device or object using signals from satellites in the outdoors.
- **Indoor Positioning System (IPS)**: This refers to locating objects or people within a building or indoor space using technologies like Bluetooth, RFID, or Wi-Fi, since GPS signals may be weak or unavailable indoors.

In both cases, the goal of localization is to determine and sometimes track a precise geographic position, which can be used for navigation, location-based services, or other location-aware applications.

3.1.1 Geographical Positioning System

The **Geographical Positioning System (GPS)** is a satellite-based navigation system that provides precise location and time information anywhere on Earth, under any weather conditions, and at any time of day. It is commonly used for navigation, mapping, and location-based services.

Here's a breakdown of the key components and functionality of GPS:

Key Components of GPS

1. Satellites

- The GPS system consists of a constellation of at least **24 satellites** orbiting the Earth. These satellites continuously broadcast signals containing their location and the exact time the signal was sent.

2. Ground Control Stations

- Ground control stations monitor and manage the GPS satellites. They track the satellites' positions, maintain their correct orbits, and ensure the system is working accurately.

3. Receivers (e.g., smartphones, car navigation systems)

- GPS receivers, which are found in devices like smartphones, cars, and other navigation equipment, receive the signals from the satellites. The receiver then processes this information to determine its position (latitude, longitude, altitude) and time.

How GPS Works

1. Triangulation/Trilateration

- GPS determines your position by measuring the distance to multiple satellites. This is done by calculating how long it takes for the GPS signal to travel from the satellite to the receiver.
- With at least **four satellites**, the receiver can calculate its 3D position (latitude, longitude, and altitude) by using **trilateration**—a process that involves intersecting spheres centered around each satellite's location.

2. Time Signal

- The GPS satellites continuously broadcast signals that include the time at which they were sent, according to atomic clocks onboard the satellites.
- By comparing the time the signal was sent with the time it was received (which is tracked by the receiver), the GPS device calculates the distance to each satellite.

3. Calculating Position

- Using the time delay and the position of the satellites, the receiver can determine its own position. The accuracy of the positioning is determined by factors such as the number of satellites the receiver can communicate with, atmospheric conditions, and the quality of the satellite signals.

Key Features of GPS

- **Global Coverage**: GPS provides global coverage, meaning it can be used anywhere on Earth, whether in remote areas or urban environments.
- **Real-Time Tracking**: GPS systems provide real-time location data, allowing for immediate position determination.
- **High Accuracy**: GPS can provide location accuracy within a few meters under optimal conditions. With the help of additional systems like **Differential GPS (DGPS)** or **Augmented GPS (A-GPS)**, accuracy can be further improved to within centimeters.

Applications of GPS

1. Navigation

- **In cars, ships, and airplanes**, GPS is used for real-time navigation, helping users reach their destinations efficiently.

2. Mapping and Surveying

- GPS is widely used for geographic mapping and land surveying, offering precise coordinates for creating accurate maps and planning urban development.

3. Location-Based Services (LBS)

- Apps like Google Maps, Uber, or fitness trackers rely on GPS to provide location-specific services such as directions, real-time traffic data, and ride-sharing.

4. Search and Rescue

- GPS is essential for locating people in emergency situations, such as hikers or boaters who are lost or in distress.

5. Military and Defense

- GPS is crucial for military operations, including navigation, precision targeting, and strategic planning.

6. Agriculture

- GPS-based technologies help farmers with precision farming, allowing them to map fields, track equipment, and optimize the use of resources like water and fertilizers.

7. Tracking and Fleet Management

- Businesses use GPS to monitor vehicles, shipments, and assets in real-time, enhancing logistics, delivery, and asset management.

Limitations of GPS

1. Signal Obstructions

- GPS signals can be blocked or reflected by buildings, trees, or mountains, especially in urban environments (known as the "urban canyon" effect), leading to less accurate positioning.

2. Dependence on Satellite Signals

- GPS relies entirely on satellite signals, so if the signals are weak or unavailable (e.g., in tunnels or indoors), the GPS receiver may not work effectively.

3. Atmospheric Interference

- The Earth's atmosphere, especially the ionosphere and troposphere, can cause slight errors in GPS signal transmission, which can reduce accuracy.

3.1.2 Indoor Positioning System

An **Indoor Positioning System (IPS)** is a technology used to determine the location of objects or people inside a building or other enclosed spaces, where traditional GPS signals are weak or unavailable. Unlike GPS, which relies on signals from satellites, indoor positioning systems use a combination of various technologies to calculate positions accurately within buildings.

How Indoor Positioning Systems Work

- **Signal Measurement**: Devices in the system (e.g., smartphones, wearables) receive signals from fixed beacons, Wi-Fi access points, or other infrastructure. The system then measures signal strengths, time of flight, or other metrics.
- **Position Calculation**: Based on these measurements, algorithms (like triangulation, trilateration, or fingerprinting) estimate the device's location inside the building.
- **Real-time Data Processing**: The system continuously updates the position as the user moves through the indoor environment, providing real-time location tracking.

Key Technologies Used in Indoor Positioning Systems

3.1.3 Device-based Positioning

Device-based positioning refers to systems where the object or individual being tracked **actively carries or uses a device** (such as a smartphone, wearable, or RFID tag) that communicates with the positioning infrastructure to determine its location.

Key Characteristics

- **Active Participation**: The device being tracked needs to be equipped with a positioning-capable technology, such as GPS, Bluetooth, Wi-Fi, or RFID.
- **Accuracy**: Typically, device-based systems can achieve relatively high accuracy, often down to a few meters or even centimeters, depending on the technology used.
- **Tracking Mode**: The tracked device (e.g., a smartphone or RFID tag) communicates its position through signals (e.g., Bluetooth, Wi-Fi, or GPS) to base stations, beacons, or sensors in the environment.
- **User Control**: The user or object being tracked has control over whether the tracking is enabled or disabled, as it relies on the device being worn or carried.

3.1.4 Wifi Based Localization

Wi-Fi positioning, also known as Wi-Fi-based localization or indoor positioning, is used to determine the location of a device or person within an indoor environment using Wi-Fi signals. A wireless indoor positioning system using Wi-Fi relies on the presence of access points (APs) or routers emitting wireless signals.

Each Wi-Fi access point relays data allowing internet access. Wi-Fi positioning can take advantage of signals emitted from Wi-Fi routers to gain some insights into a user's location.

How Does Wi-Fi Positioning Work?

When a Wi-Fi router sends a wireless signal, Wi-Fi receivers, such as smartphones and tablets, can accept those signals. Each signal contains some metadata which can be processed and used to determine a user's location.

Wi-Fi metadata:

- MAC address (unique ID for the router)
- Received Signal Strength (RSS)
- Channel State Information (CSI)

Using these metadata, the position can be calculated in 2 ways,

- **WiFi trilateration** uses the location of each Wi-Fi router. Then, based on the RSS or CSI, it estimates a distance between a user and each visible Wi-Fi router to calculate its position based on those distances.
- **Wi-Fi fingerprinting** does not need to know Wi-Fi router locations, but instead creates a large fingerprint map of what the RSS of each MAC address looks like at various locations and then in real-time compares the measured RSS to the fingerprint map to determine a user's position.

3.2 WIFI LATERATION

Lateration is a technique used for positioning or determining the location of an object or device by measuring distances from multiple known reference points. In lateration, the **distance** to at least three (or more) fixed points (reference points) is used to calculate the exact position of a target. It requires,

1. **Reference Points (Anchors):** These are the fixed points whose positions are known in advance. They can be physical objects like WiFi access points, GPS satellites, or other sensors that have a known location.
2. **Distance Measurement:** The distance between the target and each of the reference points is measured. The more accurate these distance measurements are, the more precise the resulting position calculation will be. The distance measurement is done either using the RSSI or CSI measurement.
3. **Positioning:** Using the distance measurements, a system of geometric equations is created to solve for the target's position (usually in 2D or 3D space).

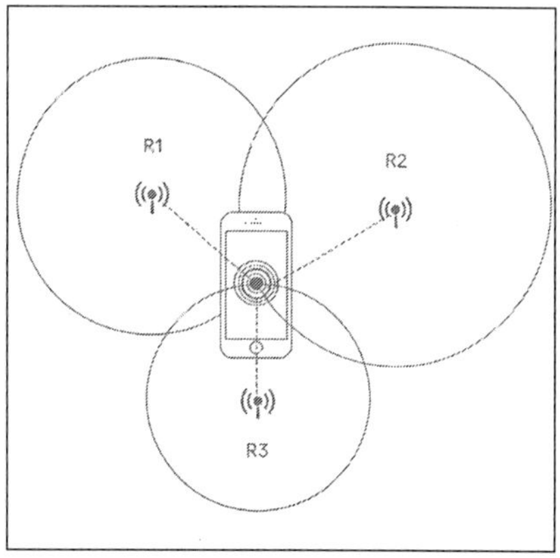

Fig. 3.1: Trilateration

It uses the known distance of at least three fixed points in 2D space (Trilateration). Trilateration works by finding a series of circles that intersect with each other. A minimum of four fixed points is used in 3D space to determine an object's position (Multilateration).

3.2.1 Wifi Fingerprinting

WiFi Fingerprinting is a technique used for indoor positioning and location-based services that relies on the unique characteristics of WiFi signals received at various locations within an environment. The idea is to create a "fingerprint" or signature of the WiFi signal at different locations, which can then be used to estimate the position of a device by comparing its received WiFi signal with these pre-recorded fingerprints. The pre-recorded fingerprints are stored in a database in the offline mode and are matched in the online mode. Fingerprint data may be one of the meta data already specified.

This method consists of 2 phases.

1. Offline Data Collection Phase

Indoor space is divided into Access point and Reference Point. Wireless APs are first deployed in the building and are labelled as AP1, AP2, ... , APn. By scanning the AP signals at the reference point in the environment with a smart terminal, the signals that are emitted from different APs and the corresponding MAC addresses that are associated with these APs can be obtained. The intensity of the received signals is represented by the RSS. During propagation, the WiFi signal will experience a path loss. Specifically, the power density of the signal decreases with an increase in the distance that follows the path loss model. The intensity of the WiFi signal emitted from the same AP becomes unique at different travelling distances. Each location is represented by a unique RSS vector (RSSi1, RSSi2, ... , RSSin) based on the signals emitted from multiple APs. This one-to-one relationship between the

RSS vector and the location is similar to the concept of a human fingerprint, and can be used as a unique identifier of the location information. Therefore, the RSS vector measured at a specific location can be used to predict its actual geological position. . By collecting the intensity data of the WiFi signals emitted from different APs at these reference points, we can construct the RSS vector of the reference point with the components of the vector that follow the same order of the AP sequence. These RSS vectors, along with the coordinates of the reference points, can be stored together in the database. Subsequently, an indoor fingerprint database (radio map) is constructed.

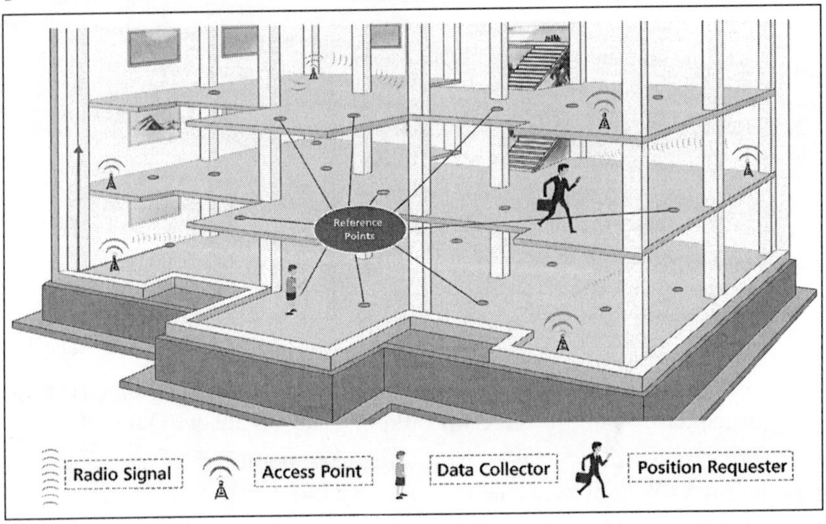

Fig. 3.2

2. Online Finger Print Matching Phase

By comparing and matching the RSS vector of a target location with the data in the fingerprint database, we can determine the position of the target location.

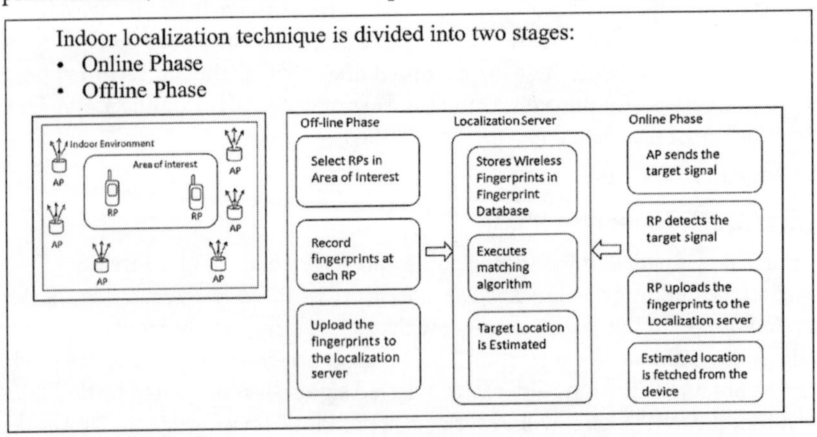

Fig. 3.3

3.2.2 Localization Server

It holds the Fingerprint database and executes the matching algorithm.

Localization Using RSSI

The Received Signal Strength Indicator (RSSI) ranging-based localization algorithm is a straightforward and economically viable localization method that utilizes RSSI measurements to determine distances in the sensor node positions in reference to the transmitter node. The positioning system calculates the strength of a radio signal that the device has received. . If a transmitter is moved closer to a receiver, the strength of the transmitted signal increases at the receiving antenna. Otherwise, the signal strength at the receiving antenna decreases if a transmitter is moved further away. RSSI is measured in dBm, with a higher negative value (in dBm) indicating a weaker signal. Radio signals that use RSSI as one of the measurements are Bluetooth Low Energy protocol (BLE) and Wi-Fi IEEE 802.11 standard.

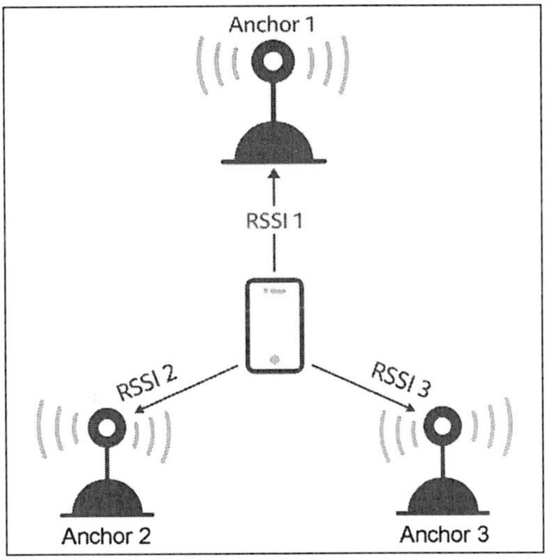

Fig. 3.4

The RSSI based positioning model is a radio-propagation model that predicts the path loss a signal encounters inside a building or densely populated area. However, due to the strong reflections and scattering conditions indoors, RSSI measurements are seriously attenuated. Therefore, it is a challenging task to accurately estimate the position with RSSI measurements and the path loss model has given the various fading effects. Hence CSI based measurements are widely used.

Metric	RSSI	CSI
Network layer	MAC layer	Physical layer
Time resolution	Packet size	Multipath signal cluster scale
Frequency resolution	No	Subcarrier scale
Temporal stability	Low	High
Measurement band	RF band	Base band
Granularity	Coarse-grained (per packet)	Fine-grained (per subcarrier)
University	Almost all Wi-Fi devices	Some Wi-Fi devices

3.3 CHANNEL STATE INFORMATION (CSI)

CSI represents the characteristics of the wireless channel, including how a signal propagates from the transmitter to the receiver. Recent studies demonstrate that CSI outperforms RSSI in sensing accuracy due to its stability and rich information. The CSI can fully reflect the multipath effect of the physical environment, which is more fine-grained than the RSS. CSI contains the values of Amplitude, Phase, and Frequency. The CSI based localization also follows fingerprinting and lateration method. The Fingerprinting based architecture is described below.

3.3.1 Data Collection

Collecting stable and reliable data is the first step in a fingerprinting-based approach, and both the offline and online phases start with data collection. In the offline phase, the user was asked to stand at different locations known as Reference Points.

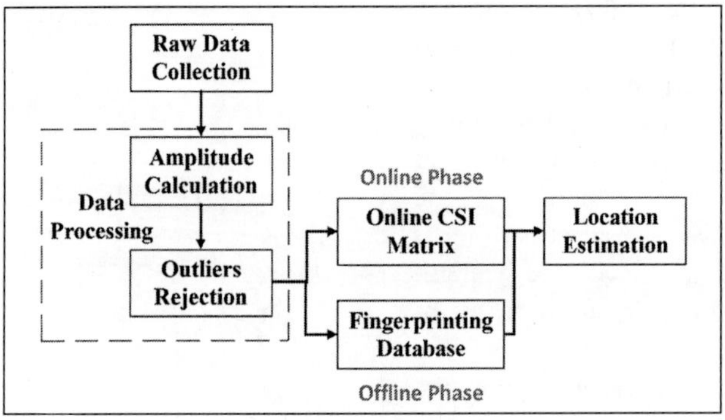

Fig. 3.5

3.3.2 Data Processing

Direct use of the raw CSI can lead to an error in localization due to the effect of interference, so the data must be processed. The data processing consisted of two parts: amplitude calculation and outlier rejection.

3.3.3 Amplitude Calculation

Reasons such as the lack of clock synchronization between the transmitter and receiver, the mismatch between transmitter and receiver frequencies, and the noise interference make the original phase of the CSI subject to error and cannot be used as the feature to distinguish locations. The amplitude of the CSI is more stable than the phase in a stationary environment, so the amplitude was chosen as the key feature to distinguish locations

3.3.4 Outlier Rejection

Outliers are values that significantly differ from other values in the dataset. During our data collection process, the CSI of each location was measured several times, and using this criterion, highly abnormal outliers could be removed, after which, the average of the data needed to be calculated again to obtain the true amplitude.

3.3.5 Establishment of Fingerprint Database

In this part, a correspondence between the CSI and the location needed to be established so that the locations of the test points could be located based on the fingerprint database during the online phase.

3.3.6 Fine Timing Measurement Protocol

Fine Timing Measurement (FTM) Protocol is a feature introduced in the IEEE 802.11. It provides Wi-Fi positioning that relies on the Time of Flight of the signal instead of its received strength. Time of flight information is supposed to be more reliable compared to signal strength, providing more accurate distance estimates to be used in positioning. FTM is claimed to provide meter-level positioning accuracy.

3.3.7 FTM Protocol Structure

The FTM protocol consists of the following key steps and exchanges:

1. FTM Measurement Request (Initiator)

- The device (client) sends an **FTM Measurement Request** to the access point. This request includes the parameters for the measurement, such as the desired accuracy or the timing window for the exchange.

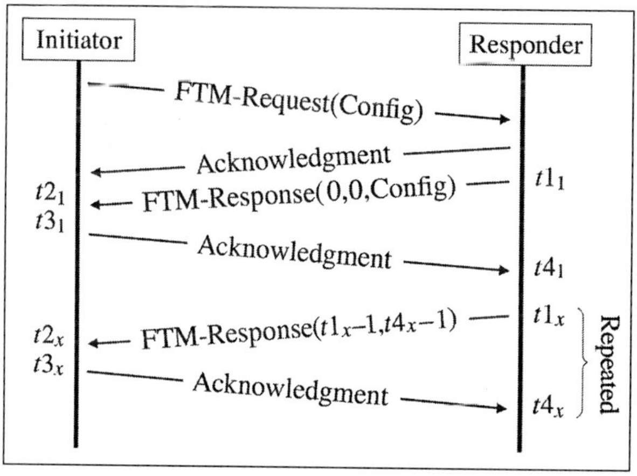

Fig. 3.6

2. FTM Measurement Response (Responder)

- The AP replies to the FTM Measurement Request with an **FTM Measurement Response**, which includes its timestamp of when it received the request.

3. FTM Measurement Confirmation (Initiator)

- The device responds with a **Measurement Confirmation**, indicating that it has received the FTM Response and also providing its timestamp when it received the response from the AP.

4. RTT Calculation

- After these exchanges, both the device and the AP have the necessary timestamps to calculate the **round-trip time (RTT)**.
- The RTT can then be used to calculate the **distance** between the device and the AP using the formula: d=c×RTT2d = \frac{c \times RTT}{2}d=2c×RTT where ccc is the speed of light, and RTTRTTRTT is the round-trip time.

5. Distance Estimation

- The device now knows its distance to the AP and can use the measurements from multiple APs (if available) for further positioning, triangulation, or multilateration.

3.3.8 Smart Phone Based Localization Using Sensors

Built-in sensors for smartphones include accelerometers, gyroscopes, magnetometers, barometers, light intensity sensors, cameras, microphones, etc. These sensors are not designed for positioning, but measurements from such sensors can be used for indoor positioning with proprietary methods.

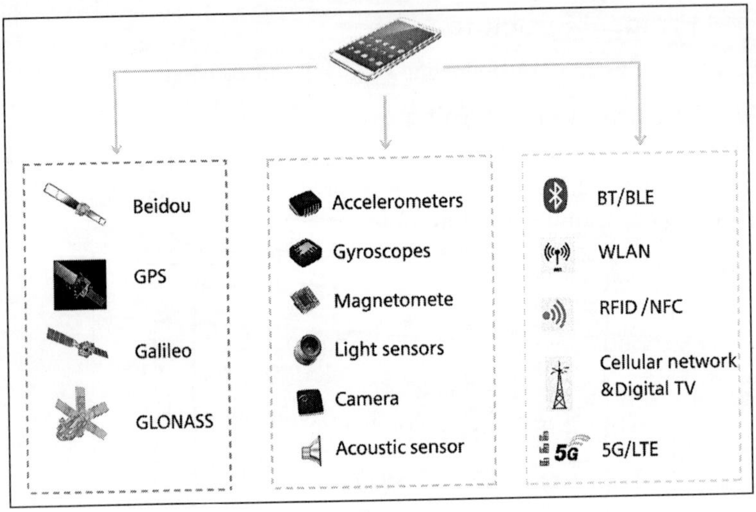

Fig. 3.7

Category	Sensor technology	(+) Advantages (–) Disadvantages
Vision-based	Video camera	+ Effective security measure + Maintain records – Interface with privacy – Interface with privacy – Interface with privacy
Motion-based	Accelerometer Gyroscopes PIR	+ No privacy issue + Lower cost (PIR) + High detection accuracy – Raise physical discomfort issue (accelerometer and gyroscopes) – No direct linear or angular position information – Low range and line-of-sight restriction (PIR) – Prone to false detection – Insensitive to very slow motions
Sound-based	Ultrasonic Acoustic Audio (microphone)	+ Very sensitive to motion + Objects and distances are typically determined precisely + Inexpensive (audio) – Work only directionally (ultrasonic) – Sensitive to temperature and angle of the target (ultrasonic) – Easily be influenced by other audio signals/ noise – Prone to false detection – Range limited

Category	Sensor technology	(+) Advantages (–) Disadvantages
Sensor-based	Body-worn sensors (Body sensor networks)	+ High detection accuracy + No privacy issue – Expensive devices – Disturb or limit the activities of the users – Required sensors installation and calibration.

3.4 DEVICE-FREE LOCALIZATION (DFL)

In Device-free localization, the system can detect the presence and location of people or objects without requiring them to carry or wear any specific tracking device. Instead, it uses the radio signals emitted by the 5G network and the way they interact with the environment to infer the target's position.

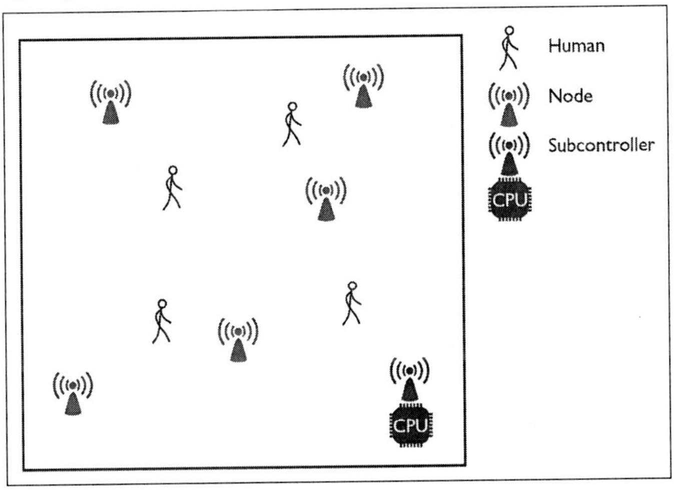

Fig. 3.8

The concept of DFL relies on the fact that any changes on the radio network environment will fluctuate the received signal profiles, i.e., due to reflection, diffraction, absorption, or scattering phenomena. It works by using RF fluctuations as an indicator of presence of obstruction, i.e., object or human.

Multiple human targets are present in an environment in which several RF nodes have been installed. Depending on the specific setup, these nodes can be transmitters, receivers or transceivers. One of the nodes acts as a (sub)controller node which regulates communication within the network and captures the desired characteristics from this RF communication. The captured data is sent to some type of processing unit (a laptop, a NUC, ...) where it is stored and/or used as input to a DFL algorithm. This algorithm will utilize the impact of the human presence on RF communication within the network for detection, tracking and/or identification of the targets.

Detection refers to the ability of a tagless localization system to detect if there are any changes in an environment caused by non-static entities and if so, estimate how many entities are causing these changes.

Tracking is to be interpreted as the continuous estimation of positions and velocities of the detected entities. This aspect tends to be focused on the most in DFL systems.

Finally, identification refers to the system's ability to determine the identity of the non-static entities. Identity in this context is a loosely interpretable term and can refer to the size, shape, material or type of an entity or to an actual human identity.

Key Characteristics

- **Tag Free**: People or objects do not need to carry any device. The system uses sensors and infrastructure to passively track their location. The area contains both
- **Context Awareness**: The system detects patterns or anomalies in the environment to infer location or movement with respect to required context. Eg. Fall detection is identified as a threat in elderly care.

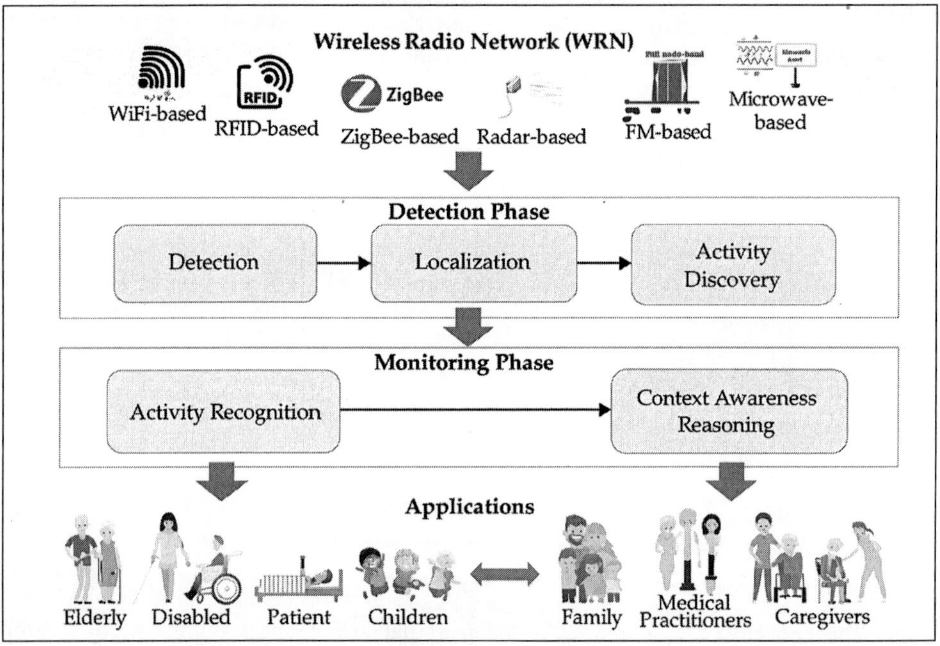

Fig. 3.9

- **Accuracy**: Device-free systems tend to have lower accuracy compared to device-based systems, often within a range of several meters to tens of meters, depending on the technology.
- **Privacy and Security**: Since the system doesn't require a personal device, device-free positioning may be preferred in environments where privacy is a concern or where individuals cannot carry devices.

3.4.1 Applications of Localization

Smartphone localization refers to the process of determining the geographic location of a smartphone and adapting its services and features based on that location. This process is essential for enabling a variety of location-based services (LBS) such as navigation, location-aware apps, social media check-ins, and more.

Smartphones use a combination of technologies to achieve accurate localization:

1. Global Positioning System (GPS)

- **GPS** is the primary method for determining the location of smartphones outdoors. It uses signals from a network of satellites to calculate the device's position with a high level of accuracy, typically within a few meters. GPS is especially useful for outdoor navigation and mapping applications.

2. Wi-Fi Positioning System (WPS)

- In urban environments or indoors where GPS signals may be weak or unavailable, smartphones use **Wi-Fi positioning** to estimate location. The phone connects to nearby Wi-Fi networks, and by comparing signal strengths and known locations of Wi-Fi access points, the device can estimate its position with reasonable accuracy.

3. Bluetooth Low Energy (BLE)

- For **indoor localization**, smartphones can use Bluetooth, specifically **Bluetooth Low Energy (BLE)**. BLE beacons placed within a building or facility transmit signals that the smartphone can pick up. By measuring the signal strength from different beacons, the device can triangulate its position.

4. Cellular Network Triangulation

- When GPS and Wi-Fi signals aren't available, smartphones can rely on **cell tower triangulation**. This method uses nearby cell towers to determine the device's location by measuring the signal strength from multiple towers. Although this method is less accurate than GPS, it can still provide a general location in areas with cellular coverage.

5. Inertial Navigation System (INS)

- Smartphones also use **accelerometers, gyroscopes**, and **magnetometers** (motion sensors) to detect movement and orientation. This **inertial navigation system** (INS) can help estimate the position of the smartphone when other localization methods (like GPS) are unavailable, especially in indoor or obstructed environments.

6. Sensor Fusion

- To improve accuracy and overcome limitations of individual technologies, smartphones often use **sensor fusion** techniques. This means combining data from GPS, Wi-Fi, Bluetooth, accelerometers, and other sensors to provide a more accurate and reliable location estimate. For example, if GPS signals are weak, accelerometer data can be used to track movement.

3.4.2 Applications of Smartphone Localization

1. **Navigation and Maps**: GPS is commonly used for apps like Google Maps or Apple Maps, providing driving, walking, and public transportation directions.
2. **Location-based Services (LBS)**: These include services like weather apps, nearby restaurant recommendations, and location-based ads. For example, ride-sharing apps like Uber or Lyft use smartphone localization to match users with nearby drivers.

3. **Social Media**: Apps like Facebook, Instagram, and Snapchat allow users to share their current location, check-in at places, or tag posts with geographic data.
4. **Geofencing**: Geofencing allows apps to trigger actions when a user enters or exits a predefined location. For example, a store app might send a promotion notification when a user is near the store.
5. **Fitness and Tracking Apps**: Apps like Strava and Runkeeper use GPS to track your running, cycling, or hiking routes.
6. **Augmented Reality (AR)**: AR apps like Pokémon Go rely heavily on accurate localization to place virtual objects in the real world based on the phone's GPS data.

Privacy Concerns

Since smartphone localization can reveal detailed information about a user's whereabouts, there are privacy concerns. Many apps request access to location data, and users must be cautious about which apps are granted permission to track their location. Modern operating systems like Android and iOS have introduced stricter privacy controls, allowing users to manage when and how their location data is shared.

3.5 BACKSCATTER COMMUNICATION

Backscatter communication is a low-power wireless communication technique where a device (backscatter tag) transmits data by modulating and reflecting existing signals (like Wi-Fi or Bluetooth) back to a receiver, without needing its own active transmitter. Backscatter method uses an incident Radio-Frequency (RF) signal to transmit data without a power source.

It employs passive reflection and modulation of the incoming RF signal and converts into tens or hundreds of microwatts of electricity, that can be encoded for data communications. It differs from other wireless networks since the communication is half duplex in nature, i.e., both the sender and receiver cannot transmit at once. The mains advantage is that it's low energy requirements and low complexity of deployment.

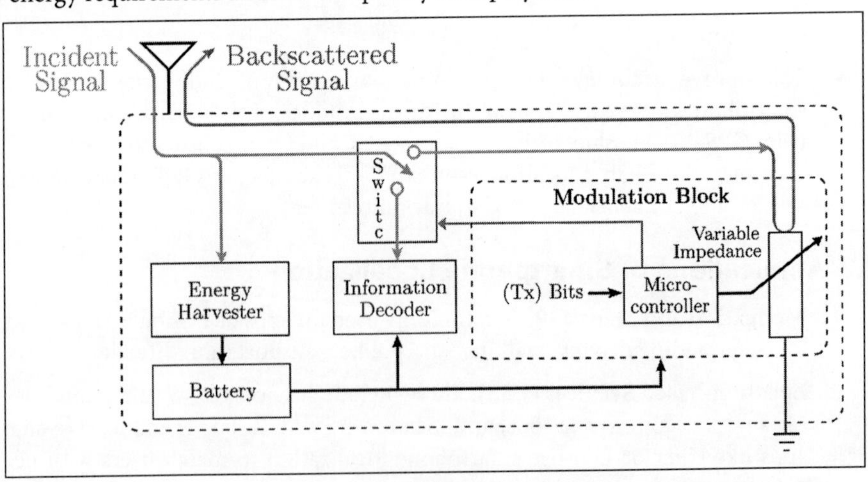

Fig. 3.10: The architecture of a backscatter tag

The architecture of the tag consists of an RF energy-harvesting block, a battery, a modulation block, and an information decoder. The tag is a passive node that harvests energy from an incident single-tone sinusoidal continuous wave (CW) radiated by the reader, and also modulates and reflects a fraction of the wave back to the reader. Specifically, the wave reflection is due to an intentional mismatch between the antenna and load impedance. Varying the load impedance makes the reflection coefficient to vary following a random sequence that modulates the reflected wave with tag's information bits. Such a modulation scheme is named as the *backscatter modulation*. The passive tag is powered by RF energy harvesting and does not require any active RF component.

A basic backscatter communication system has two main components.

- **Tags** are encoded with a unique ID and are affixed on moving objects so that they canbe identified or tracked. Tags are passive nodes that don't have their own power source. The architecture of the tag consists of an RF energy-harvesting block, a battery, amodulation block, and an information decoder.
- **Readers** are the intelligent part of the system that are installed at tracking points to read information from tags when they come into range. The reader always transmits a signal as a single-tone sinusoidal continuous wave, regardless of whether it has bits to send or not. The reader has its own power supply and a full set of conventional RF components for emitting CW and information transmission/ reception.

When the tag has data to send, it harvests the signal received from the reader get the power to run. To send bits, it modulates the incident signal to encode its data and then reflects a fractionof the wave back to the reader. This method is called backscattering. In general, the communication between the reader and the tag has two modes:

Forward Information Transmission, i.e., The Reader-to-Tag Transmission

For the forward information transmission, the reader transmits a binary intensity modulated signal to the tag. The tag connects its information decoder and utilizes the received RF signalfor RF energy harvesting and energy-detection-based demodulation. For example, the decoded bit is "1" or "0" when a high or a low signal energy is detected, respectively. Theuse of this primitive on/off modulation and energy detection is due to the constraint that a typical tag is provisioned with an energy detector instead of a power hungry RF chain neededfor coherent demodulation.

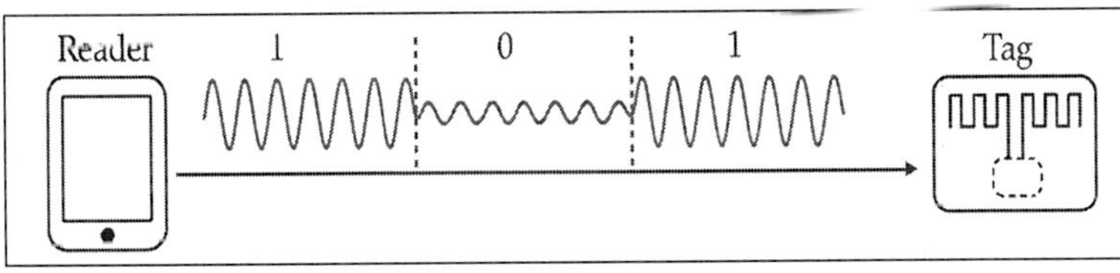

Fig. 3.11: *The forward information-transmission mode of a BackCom link*

Backward Information Transmission, i.e., The Tag-to-Reader Transmission

For the backward information transmission, the reader sends a CW signal to the tag, and the tag connects its modulation block and utilizes the received RF signal for RF energy harvesting and backscatter modulation. Generally, a tag can modulate the reflected signal by switching over a given set of impedances, generating a set of reflection coefficients forming a constellation.

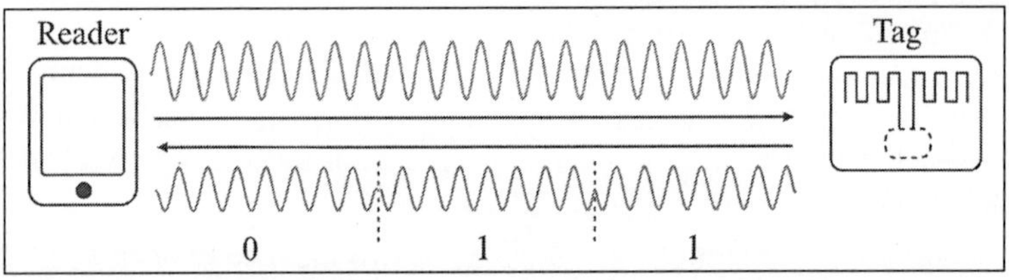

Fig. 3.12: *The backward information-transmission mode of a BackCom link*

3.5.1 Types of Backscattering

Traditional Backscattering

In a traditional backscatter communication system, data is transmitted by a tag (or node) reflecting a portion of a received signal back to a reader, modulated with the data using simpler modulation schemes like ON OFF Keying, without the tag needing its own active RF components.

Conventional Backscattering

In conventional backscattering communication systems, there are two special features that differ from traditional communication systems. First, in conventional backscattering communication systems, the receivers (i.e., WTRDs) have to be equipped with a power source to transmit RF signals to the transmitter (i.e., WTDs). Second, the transmitters do not need to be equipped witha power source to transmit data because they will reflect signals received by the receivers insteadof generating their own signals. The second feature is the most important characteristic and also the main objective for the development of conventional backscattering communication systems.

This special communication feature of CBCSs has received a great deal of attention, mainly because of the successful implementation of RFID systems and the potential use in sensor devices that are small in size and have a low power supply. Typically, backscattering communication systems operate using RF signals and require the WTRD to be able to transmit.

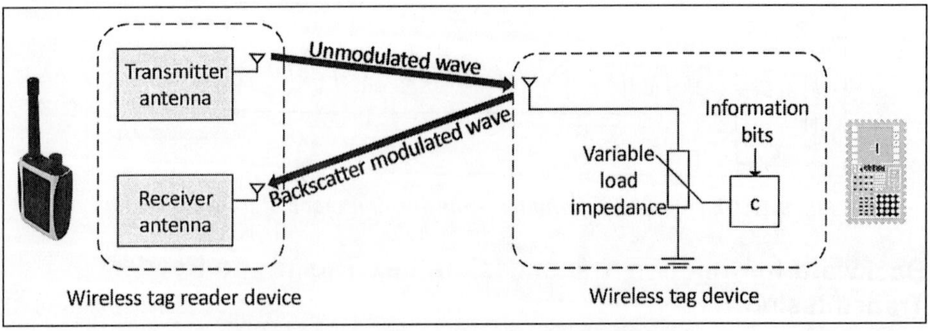

Fig. 3.13: *Conventional backscattering*

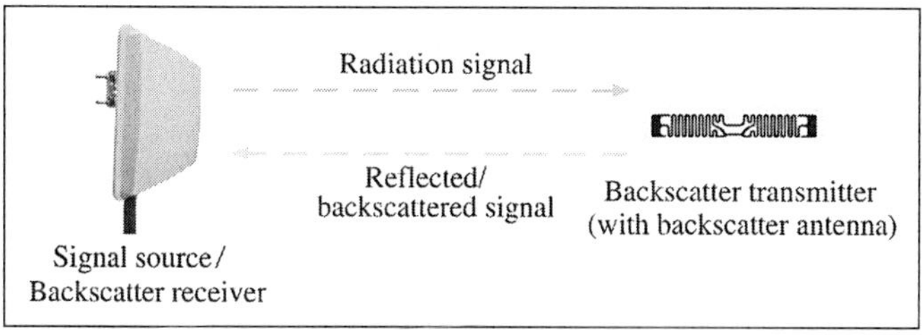

Fig. 3.14

Monostatic Backscattering

The monostatic backscatter communications, the signal source and the backscatter receiver are in the same device. In the monostatic backscatter communications, the incident signal from the signal source propagates to the backscatter transmitter as an excitation signal and then the transmitter modulates the transmit information and reflects it to the backscatter receiver. One of the most popular applications of the monostatic backscatter is the RFID, where the backscatter transmitter and the receiver are called RFID tag and the RFID reader, respectively.

In the typical monostatic backscatter system, RFID, there are three types of backscatter transmitters: active, passive, and semi-passive ones.

Backscatter transmitters	Features
Active	With internal power supply and transceiver, be able to transmit data actively, long communication range.
Passive	Without internal power, power excitation and operation via energy harvesting, with simple structure, small size, and low cost
Semi-passive	With internal power supply, usually transmit data only when being excited with advantages of both active and passive transmittes.

- The active RFID tag has the internal power supply and transceiver implemented, which can send information to the reader actively as well as backscatter the RF signal from the RFID reader.
- On the other hand, the passive tag does not have the internal power supply configured and transmits data only if the harvested energy from the reader satisfies its working requirement.
- The semi-passive tag has the compromise functions of the active and passive tags, where it has both limited power supply and energy harvesting. To save the power, the semi-passive tag doesnot transmit data actively and only transmits data when being excited. After being excited, it can use the internal power for data transmission.

Bistatic Backscattering

Bistatic scatter dislocate the carrier emitter from the reader. For the bistatic backscatter communications, the signal source and the receiver are at different terminals, where the signal source can be a dedicated signal generator or an ambient signal source. In the traditional bistatic backscatter communication system, the special carrier emitter is utilized as the signal source, which can be placed near the backscatter transmitter. Therefore, it avoids the two-way pathloss problem in the monostatic backscatter communication system and improves the system performance due to the flexibility of the special carrier emitter.

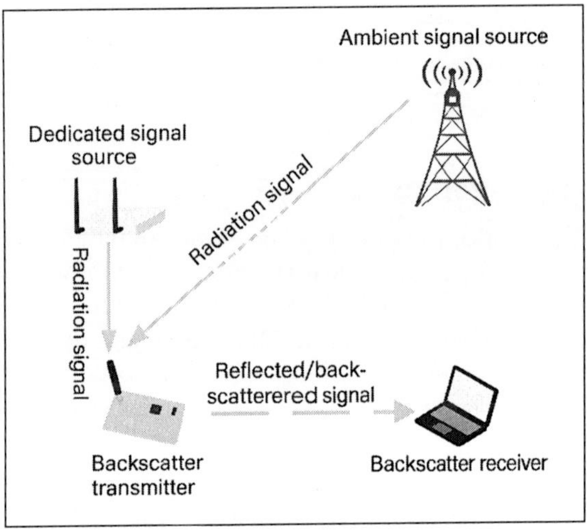

Fig. 3.15

Multiple-access Backscattering

Many real-life applications can be modeled as multiple-access (MAC) BackCom system wherea single reader serves multiple tags. For instance, in a warehouse, an administrator can use a single reader to collect information simultaneously from hundreds or thousands of items equipped with RFID tags. In a smart city, a data aggregator can receive sensing data from a large number of backscatter sensors at the same time.

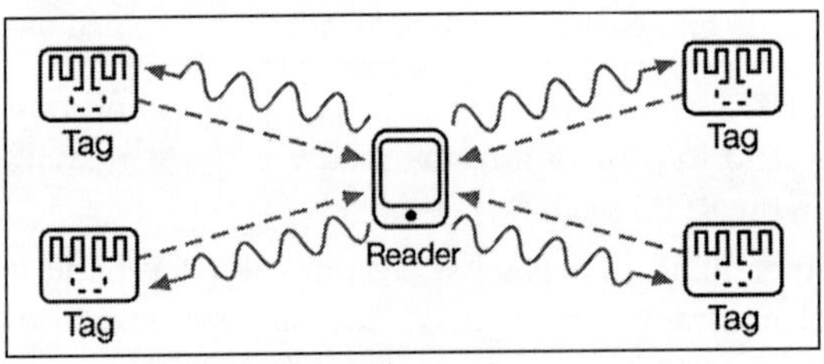

Fig. 3.16

The key challenge in multiple-access BackCom systems is how to deal with collisions that arise as a result of concurrent tag transmissions. In this regard, a simple solution is to avoid collisions between multi-tag transmissions using the traditional MAC schemes including space/frequency/code/time-division multiple-access (SDMA/FDMA/CDMA/TDMA).

Adhoc Backscattering

Ad hoc Backscatter Communication is an emerging concept in wireless communication, particularly in the context of the Internet of Things (IoT) and wireless sensor networks.

It refers to a backscatter communication network that is self-organizing and can be set up on-demand (i.e., in an "ad hoc" fashion) without relying on a pre-established infrastructure. This allows devices to communicate with each other or with other systems by reflecting existing RF signals in an organized way, without requiring a fixed base station or central hub.

Dedicated Backscattering

Dedicated Backscatter Communication refers to a type of backscatter system where the backscatter device operates in a way that it is specifically designed to communicate using a dedicated infrastructure or signal source. Unlike ad hoc backscatter communication, which forms self-organizing networks, dedicated backscatter systems rely on a fixed, pre-established transmitter or source that continuously provides the RF signals the backscatter devices reflect and modulate. This creates a communication system where the backscatter devices are specifically optimized to interact with a dedicated infrastructure or RF source to relay information.

Ambient Backscattering

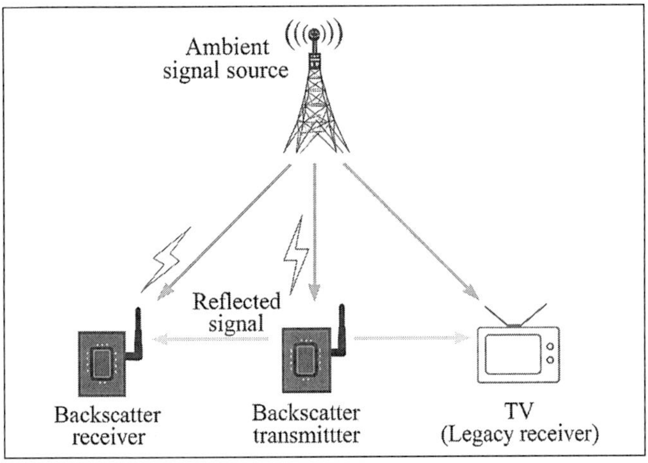

Fig. 3.17

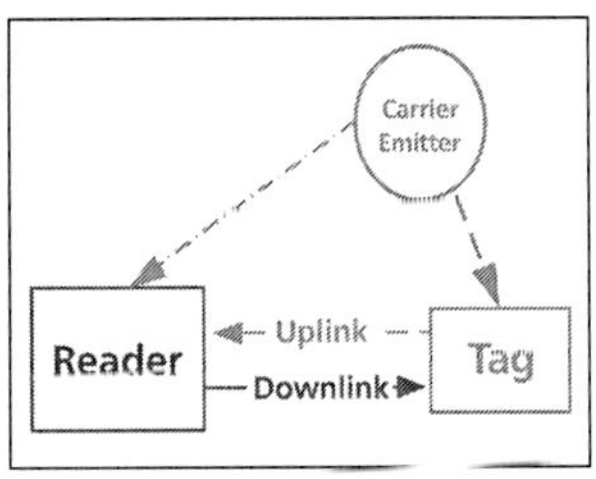

Fig. 3.18

In the ambient backscatter system, the ambient signal sources, such as cellular signals, Wi-Fi signals, TV tower signals, etc., are exploited. No dedicated signal source, such as special carrier emitter, is needed for the system. The intended receiver is termed as the legacy receiver and the BackCom devices also use the signal for their transmission.Ambient backscatter is a method of networking by way of alternately reflecting and absorbing radio frequencies (RF) in an environment.

3.5.2 Energy Harvesting In Tags

Energy harvesting in applications involving use of active RF sensors and ID tags. Unlike passive tags, active tags utilize a battery to emit rather than reflect or backscatter RF energy. Advantages of active tags include improved range and read rate in electromagnetically unfriendly environments and improved link quality.

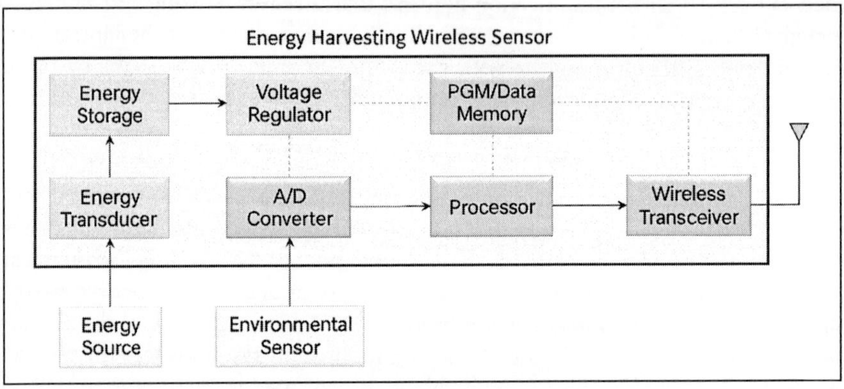

Fig. 3.19

The components of an Energy Harvesting Wireless Sensor are:

- **Energy Source:** Provides ambient energy, like solar, wind, or vibration, to be harvested.
- **Energy Transducer:** Converts the ambient energy into electrical energy. Examples include solar cells, piezoelectric devices, and electromagnetic transducers.
- **Energy Storage:** Stores the harvested energy for later use. This can be a rechargeable battery or a capacitor.
- **Voltage Regulator:** Maintains a constant voltage level to protect the electronic components from voltage fluctuations.
- **A/D Converter:** Converts the analog signal from the environmental sensor into a digital signal that can be processed by the processor.
- **Processor:** Processes the data from the A/D converter and controls the operation of the wireless sensor.
- **PGM/Data Memory:** Stores the program code and data.
- **Wireless Transceiver:** Transmits the processed data wirelessly to a central location.
- **Environmental Sensor:** Detects and measures physical parameters such as temperature, pressure, humidity, or light.

Energy harvesting wireless sensors (EHWSNs) are designed to operate autonomously by extracting energy from their surroundings. This eliminates the need for frequent battery replacements and makes them suitable for remote and inaccessible locations. These sensors are used in various applications, including environmental monitoring, industrial process monitoring, and machine health monitoring.

3.6 RFID TAGS

RFID (Radio-Frequency Identification) technology uses radio waves to identify and track objects by attaching a tag containing a microchip and antenna to them, which then communicates with a reader to transmit data.

An RFID reader sends Radio Frequency (RF) signals via an antenna. The antenna radiates the RF energy, and it is absorbed by the RFID tag attached to the object. The tag uses the absorbed energy to "power up" and return data from the embedded chip. The returned RF signal is captured by the reader's antenna and decoded by the reader. A connected system receives the decoded input for decision making.

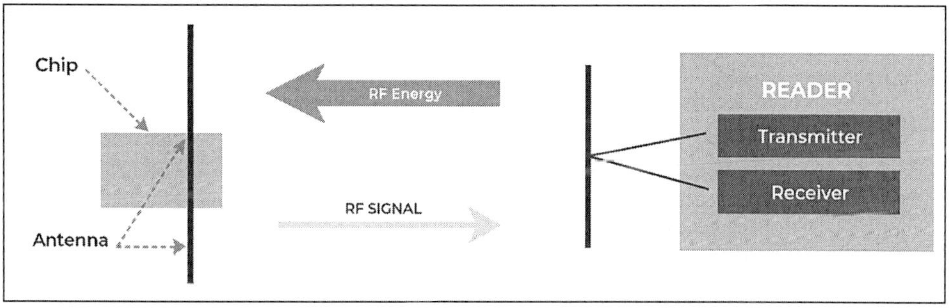

Fig. 3.20

Radio frequency (RF) sensors and tags find applications in several areas including inventory control, pallet/container tracking, identification (ID) badges and access control, fleet maintenance, equipment/personnel tracking in hospitals, parking lot access and control, car tracking in rental lots, monitoring product health in manufacturing, and so on.

3.7 INTERNET OF THINGS

The Internet of Things (IoT) refers to a network of physical devices, vehicles, appliances, and other physical objects that are embedded with sensors, software, and network connectivity, allowing them to collect and share data. Integrating 5G technology into IoT systems brings a host of benefits. With 5G's ability to support a vast number of connected devices without compromising performance, organisations can deploy more IoT sensors and devices across their operations, enabling real-time monitoring and data-driven decision-making.

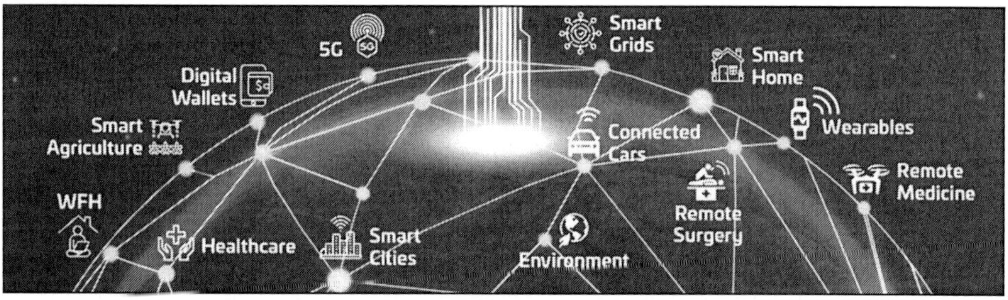

Fig. 3.21

Some of the features are:

- **High data transfer speeds:** Through higher frequency bands that allow for rapid transmission of larger data volumes.
- **Improved energy efficiency:** 5G technology enhances the energy efficiency of IoT by enabling quicker data transmission. This reduces the active operational time of these devices, leading to lower energy consumption.
- **Ultra Lower latency:** Latency in IoT refers to the time delay from when a data packet is sent from an IoT device to when it is received, processed, and an appropriate

response is generated and sent back to the device. With 5G, the response time is reduced to just a few milliseconds, enabling instantaneous decision-making and action. This reduction in delay enhances the overall performance and reliability of IoT systems.

- **Greater network reliability:** 5G ensures that IoT systems can consistently transmit and receive data, enabling real-time monitoring and control of devices.

IoT has a wide range of applications such as industry, transportation, logistics, healthcare, smart environment, personal, social gaming robot, and city information. 5G enables wireless connectivity of devices. IoT is also expressed in a multilayer model. Although some use the OSI seven-layer model with each model managed by specific protocols, others in use include the following:

- **Three-layer model:** Perception, Network and Application
- **Four-layer model:** Perception, Support, Network and Application
- **Five-layer model:** Perception, Transport, Processing, Application and Physical, DataLink, Network, Transport and Application

Perception Layer

The Perception or Physical Layer consists of the physical devices, which collect information, transformthem into digital data and pass them to another layer, so that actions can be done based on that information. Acting as a medium between the digital and real world, these physical devices can be Sensors (Temperature, Humidity, Light etc.), Actuators (Electric, Mechanical, Hydraulic etc.), RFID (RFID tags), Video Trackers (IP camera) or anything that can use data to interact with different devicesthrough a network. The difference between the traditional sensors and the smart sensors used in IoT however is that smart sensors include an integrated microprocessor (DMP), that can process the digitized data captured by the sensor. These data can be normalized, noise filtered, or transformed for the sake of signal conditioning before being forwarded to other devices throughout the network.

Transmission Layer

The Transmission Layer or Transportation or Network Layer, is located between the perception and the application layer. In this layer the data collected by smart sensors are transformed and forwarded to the Application Layer using the suitable communication channels and protocols for further processing, like analysis, data mining, data aggregation, and data encoding, while providing network management functionality and not only a basic packet routing as the network layer of the ISO/OSI model does. In IoT implementations, wireless protocols are more commonly used compared towired ones, since wireless sensors can be installed even in places that lack the main requisites for wiredsensors like power, communication cabling etc. Moreover, in a wireless sensor network, it is easier fornodes to be added, removed or relocated without reconsidering the structure of the entire network. Theselection of protocols to be used, can be based in several factors like hardware heterogeneity, power consumption, the transmission speed, and the transmission distance needed in each application and many others. In other implementations however, a wired sensor network is preferred since these networks are more reliable, more secure and offer higher transmission data speeds. For example, IoT implementations in a hospital, where reliability and speed are major factors for saving a patient's life, wired sensors arepreferable and the requisites for their installation can be planned during hospital's initial design (wiring,power delivery cables etc.). In general, smart sensors must be able to communicate with each other through Internet to handle information and interact with the physical world, while being uniquely identified to prevent data conflicts. Depending on the specific applications, smart objects can be directly reachable without the need of an intermediary gateway, implement a UI making user interaction possible and many more.

Application Layer

The Application Layer is present just above the Transmission Layer, it is based on the implementation, and can be organized in different ways. This layer, depending on the implementation, is responsible for analysing and processing the information data that came from the below Layers (Perception and Transmission). More specific, it handles these data to applications to be used for the desired actions (i.e., control actuators), acting like a bridge to transform and forward it toother nodes or hand it over to another application for further processing. Moreover, this is the layer where the user interface is placed (if any), giving the choice for users to interact with the IoT system and perform various actions (for example if a technical equipment needs servicing, the IoT will inform thetechnician through an interface that "structurally" is operating on the Application layer. The Application layer, in contrast with Transmission and Perception Layer, can vary a lot based on the implementation.Since it is designed with a desired application in mind, this layer is formed by its functionalities. For example, real-time monitoring and decision- making applications are in charge of taking actions based on the data collected from the perception layer, information digitization is responsible for collecting and transforming analog data into digital, analytics are used to process collected data and create an evaluation model, while hardware control for transforming data into physical actions.

Network Layer

In IoT architecture, the network layer is also called as transmission layer. It works bysending the data received from the perception layer to the processing unit securely. The transmission standard can be wired and wireless to send data securely and this layer use 3G, wi-fi, Bluetooth, and Zigbee technology. Thus, the data are then forwarded to the middleware layer.

Middleware Layer

One device of IoT connects to the other device only when both provide the same type of services. The middleware layer has the responsibility to connect it to the database by keeping in mindthe service management. Further, computation and decision-making are also done by the samemiddleware layer.

Business Layer

Helps in creating a business model, graph, flowchart, etc., for different business models from the output received from this layer, which is useful in determining the further business strategies.

IoT Protocol Overview

IoT protocols are an integral part of the IoT technology stack. Without IoT protocols and standards, hardware would be deemed useless. This is because IoT protocols enable hardware to exchange data. And, out of these transferred pieces of data, useful information can be extracted by the end-user. IoT protocols and standards are often overlooked when people think about the Internet of Things (IoT).

More often than not, the industry has its attention firmlyfixed upon communication. And while the interaction between devices, IOT sensors, gateways, servers, and user applications are essential components of the IoT, communication would fall down without the right IoT protocols. There are multiple IoT protocols available, with each one offering certain capabilities or combinations of features that make it preferable over otheroptions for specific IoT deployments. Each IoT protocol enables either device-to-device, device-to-gateway or device-to-cloud/data center communication -- or combinations of those communications. Factors such as geographic and special location, power consumption needs, battery-operated options, the presence of physical barriers and cost determine which protocol is optimal in an IoT deployment. IoT protocols and standards are broadly classified into two separate categories. These are:

1. IoT data protocols (Presentation / Application layers)
2. Network protocols for IoT (Datalink / Physical layers)

IoT Data Protocols

IoT data protocols are used to connect low-power IoT devices. They provide communication with hardware on the user side: without the need for any internet connection. The connectivity in IoT data protocols and standards is through a wired or cellular network. IoT data protocols were designed to tackle unreliable communication networks. This became a need in the IoT world due to the increasing number of small, cheap, and lower-power objects that have appeared in the network over the past few years.

Application layer	HTTP, CaAP, EBHTTP, LTP, SNMP, IPfix, DNS, NTP, SSH, DLMS, COSEM, DNP, MODBUS
Network/ Communication layer	Ipv6/IPv4, RPL, TCP/UDP, uIP, SLIP, 6LoWPAN,
PHY/MAC layer	IEEE 802.11 Series, 802.15 Series, 802.3, 802.16, WirelessHART, z-WAVE, UWE, IrDA, PLC, LonWorks, KNX

3.8 MQTT (MESSAGE QUEUING TELEMETRY TRANSPORT)

MQTT (Message Queuing Telemetry Transport) is a lightweight IoT data protocol developed in 1999.

One of the most preferred protocols for battery-powered IoT devices, MQTT collects data from various electronic devices and supports remote device monitoring. It has been especially designed for unreliable communication networks in order to respond to the problem of the growing number of small-sized cheap low-power objects that have made their appearance in the network in the recent years. MQTT is based on subscriber, publisher and broker model.

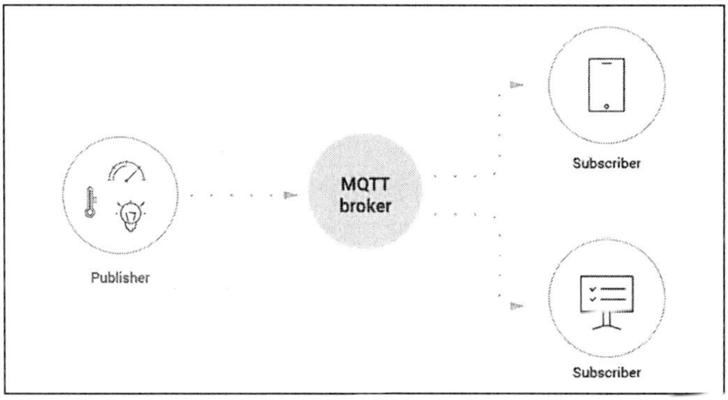

Fig. 3.22

Within the model, the publisher's task is to collect the dataand send information to subscribers via the mediation layer which is the broker. The role of the broker, on the other hand, is to ensure security by cross-checking the authorisation of publishers and subscribers. It features a publisher-subscriber messaging model and allows for simple data flow between different devices. This subscribe/publish protocol that runs over Transmission Control Protocol (TCP), which means it supports event-driven message exchange through wireless networks. MQTT is mainly used indevices which are economical and requires less power and memory.

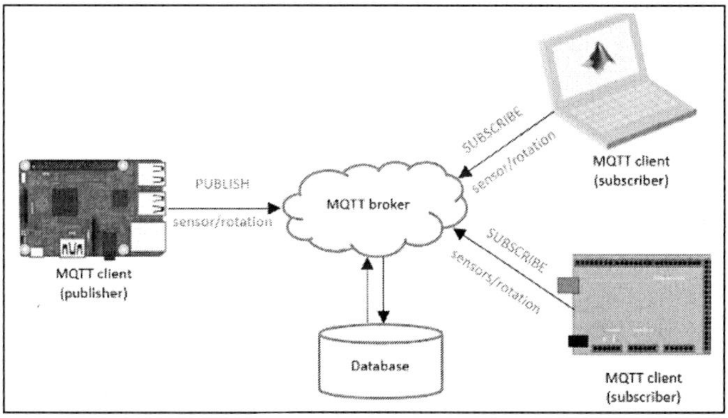

Fig. 3.23

For instance, fire detectors, car sensors, smart watches, and apps for text-based messaging. MQTT's main selling point is its architecture. Its genetic make-up is basic and lightweight and, t herefore, it's able to provide low powerconsumption for devices.

MQTT offers three modes of achieving Quality of Service, the publisher has the possibility to definethe quality of its message:

- **QoS0 (At most once):** The least reliable mode but also the fastest. The publication is sent butconfirmation is not received.
- **QoS1 (At least once):** Ensures that the message is delivered at least once, but duplicates maybe received.
- **QoS2 (Exactly once):** The most reliable mode while the most bandwidth-consuming.Duplicates are controlled to ensure that the message is delivered only once.

MQTT responds well to:

- Minimum bandwidth use
- Low energy consumption
- Little processing and memory resources
- It requires minimal resources since it is lightweight and efficient
- Support bi-directional messaging between device and cloud
- Can scale to millions of connected devices
- Support reliable message delivery through 3 QoS levels
- Works well over unreliable networks
- Security enabled, so it works with TLS and common authentication protocols

Despite its characteristics, MQTT can be problematic for some devices, due to the fact of the transmission of messages over TCP and managing long topic names. This is solved with the MQTT-SNvariant that uses UDP and supports topic name indexing. However, despite its wide adoption, MQTT doesn't support a well-defined data representation and device management structure model, which renders the implementation of its data management and device management capabilities entirely platform- or vendor-specific.

MQTT Alternatives

MQTT vs. XMPP

XMPP protocol uses XMP language and is more code-heavy and bandwidth-consuming than MQTT. It also does not use the pub/sub model by default. MQTT is therefore far superior to use than XMPP.

MQTT vs. HTTP(S)

HTTP(S) is the language of the web and thus enables communication with web applications. However, it is heavier in code use than MQTT and thus needs more power. Moreover, HTTP(S) cannot transmit many messages simultaneously, thus reducing the effectiveness of network communication.

MQTT vs. AMQP

AMQP is also a lightweight protocol. However, compared to MQTT, it is a more complex messaging system and thus uses more power and memory than MQTT.

CoAP (Constrained Application Protocol)

Created by the IETF Constrained RESTful Environments working group and launched in 2013, CoAP (Constrained Application Protocol) is an application layer protocol. It's an internet-utility protocol designed to address the needs of HTTP-based IoT systems. HTTP stands for Hypertext Transfer Protocol, and it's the foundation of data communication for the World Wide Web. Using this protocol, the client can send a request to the server and the server can send back the response to the client in HTTP. For light-weight implementation, it makes use of UDP (User Datagram Protocol) and reduces space usage. The protocol uses binary data format EXL (Efficient XML Interchanges). CoAP protocol is used mainly in automation, mobiles, and microcontrollers. The protocol sends a request to the application endpoints such as appliances at homes and sends back the response of services and resources in the application. While the existing structure of the internet is freely available and usable by any IoT device, it's often too heavy and power-consuming for most IoT applications. This has led to many within the IoT community dismissing HTTP as a protocol not suitable for IoT.However, CoAp has addressed this limitation by translating the HTTP model into usage in restrictive devices and network environments. It has incredibly low overheads, is easy to employ, and has the ability to enable multicast support.Therefore, it's ideal for use in devices with resource limitations, such as IoT microcontrollers or WSN nodes. It's traditionally used in applications involving smart energyand building automation.

Designed to address the needs of HTTP-based IoT systems, CoAP relies on the User Datagram Protocol(UDP) for establishing secure communication between endpoints. By allowing for broadcasting and multicasting, UDP is able to transmit data to multiple hosts while retaining communication speed andlow bandwidth usage, which makes it a good match for wireless networks typically employed in resource-constrained M2M environments. Another thing that CoAP shares with HTTP is the RESTfularchitecture which supports a request/response interaction model between application endpoints. Whatis more, CoAP adopts the basic HTTP get, post, put and delete methods, thanks to which ambiguity canbe avoided at the time of interaction between clients. CoAP features Quality of Service which is used tocontrol the messages sent and mark them as 'confirmable' or 'nonconfirmable' accordingly which indicates whether the recipient should return an 'ack' or not. Other interesting features of CoAP are thatit supports content negotiation and resource discovery mechanism. Apart from transferring IoT data, CoAP leverages Datagram Transport Layer Security (DTLS) for the secure exchange of messages in the transport layer. CoAP fully addresses the needs of an extremely light protocol in order to meet the demands of battery-operated or low-energy devices. All in all, CoAP is a good match when it comes toexisting web service-based IoT systems.

DTLS solves two problems:

- Reordering
- Packet lost.

It adds three implements:

- Packet retransmission
- Assigning sequence number within the handshake
- Replay detection

Unlike network layer security protocols, DTLS in application layer protects end-to-end communication. No end-to-end communication protection will make it easy for attacker to access to all text data thatpasses through a compromised node. DTLS also avoids cryptographic overhead problems that occur inlower layer security protocols.

CoAP Vs MQTT

CoAP performs better for high packet losses. CoAP messages can be transferred three times faster than HTTP messages. However, when comparing HTTP/2 with CoAP, HTTP/2 performed better in highcongestion scenarios. CoAP required less bandwidth compared to MQTT. In a network under heavy load, CoAP used less bandwidth than MQTT whereas DDS took up twice the bandwidth of MQTT. CoAP also had higher efficiency, calculated as a ratio of useful information bytes to total bytes at application and transport layers. In terms of energy consumption, both MQTT and CoAP are efficient.

MQTT is based on TCP. There's also a variant of MQTT called MQTT-SN that runs on UDP. Comparing CoAP against MQTT-SN may be more appropriate. Likewise, CoAP running on topof TCP (RFC 8323) can be compared against MQTT.

Features of CoAP Protocol

- It is very efficient RESTful protocol.
- Easy to proxy to/from HTTP.
- It is open IETF standard
- It is Embedded web transfer protocol (coap://)
- It uses asynchronous transaction model.
- UDP is binding with reliability and multicast support.
- GET, POST, PUT and DELETE methods are used.
- URI is supported.
- It uses small and simple 4 byte header.
- Supports binding to UDP, SMS and TCP.
- DTLS based PSK, RPK and certificate security is used.
- uses subset of MIME types and HTTP response codes.
- Uses built in discovery mechanism.

CoAP vs. HTTP

CoAP is network-oriented protocol, using similar features to HTTP but also allows for low overhead, multicast, etc. As HTTP protocol is a long-term successful standard, it can use small script to integratevarious resources and services. Interoperation provided by HTTP is the key point of IoT, for this, HTTP is employed in application level. However, HTTP is based on TCP protocol using point to point (p2p) communication model that not suitable for notification push services. Also, for constrained devices, HTTP is too complex. Unlike HTTP based protocols, CoAP operates over UDP instead of using complexcongestion control as in TCP. CoAP is based on REST architecture, which is a general design for accessing Internet resources. In order to overcome disadvantage in constrained resource, CoAP need to optimize the length of datagram and provide reliable communication. On one side, CoAP provides URI, REST method such as GET, POST, PUT, and DELETE. On the other side, based on lightweight UDP protocol, CoAP allows IP multicast, which satisfies group communication for IoT. To compensate for the unreliability of UDP protocol, CoAP defines a retransmission mechanism and provides resource discovery mechanism with resource descriptions. CoAP is not just a simply compression of HTTP protocol. Considering low processing capability and low power consuming demand of restrained resource, CoAP redesigned some features of HTTP to accommodate these limitations. HTTP used under unconstrained network and CoAP used under constrained network. Recently, HTTP-CoAP crossprotocol proxy arouses scientific interest, it has and important role in solving congestion problem in the constrained environment.

CoAP Structure Model

CoAP interactive model is similar to HTTP's client/server model. The bottom layer is Message layer that has been designed to deal with UDP and asynchronous switching. The request/response layer concerns communication method and deal with request/response message.

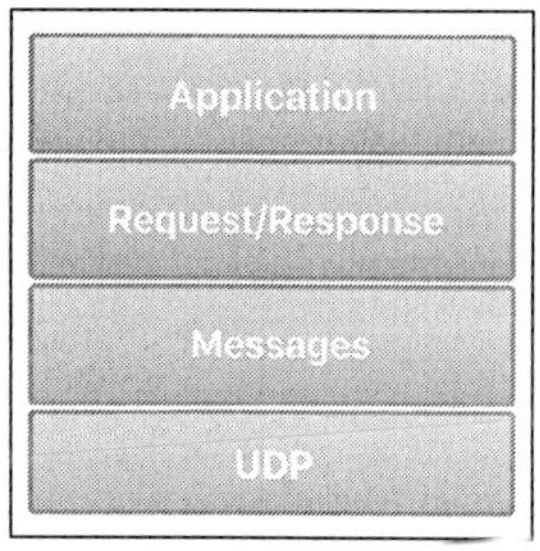

Fig. 3.24

Message Layer model

Message Layer supports 4 types message:

- CON (confirmable),
- NON (non-confirmable),
- ACK (Acknowledgement),
- RST (Reset)

(a) **Reliable message transport:** Keep retransmission until get ACK with the same message ID . Using default time out and decreasing counting time exponentially when transmitting CON. If recipient fail to process message, it responses by replacing ACK with RST.

(b) **Unreliable message transport:** transporting with NON type message. It doesn't need to be ACKed, but has to contain message ID for supervising in case of retransmission. If recipient fail to process message, server replies RST.

Request/Response Layer Model

(a) **Piggy-backed:** Client sends request using CON type or NON type message and receives response ACK with confirmable message immediately. For successful response, ACK contain response message (identify by using token), for failure response, ACK contain failure response code.

(b) **Separate response:** If server receive a CON type message but not able to response this request immediately, it will send an empty ACK in case of client resend this message. When server ready to response this request, it will send a new CON to client and client reply a confirmable message with acknowledgment. ACK is just to confirm CON message, no matter CON message carry request or response .

(c) **Non confirmable request and response:** unlike Piggy-backed response carry confirmable message, in Non confirmable request client send NON type message indicate that Server don't need to confirm. Server will resend a NON type message with response.

Features	CoAP	MQTT
Full Form	Constrained Application Protocol	Message Queue Telemetry Transport
Model used for communication	Request-Response, Publish-Subscribe	Publish-Subscribe
RESTful	Yes	No
Transport layer	Preferably UDP, TCP can also be used.	Preferably TCP, UDP can also be used (MQTT-S).
Header Size	4 Bytes	2 Bytes
Number of message types used	4	16

Features	CoAP	MQTT
Messaging	Asynchronous & Synchronous	Asynchronous
Application Reliability	2 Levels	3 Levels
Security	IPSEC or DTLS	Not defined in the standard
Intermediaries	YES	YES (MQTT-S)
LLN Suitability (thousand nodes)	Excellent	Fair
Application success stories	Utility Field Area Networks	Extending enterprise messaging into IoT

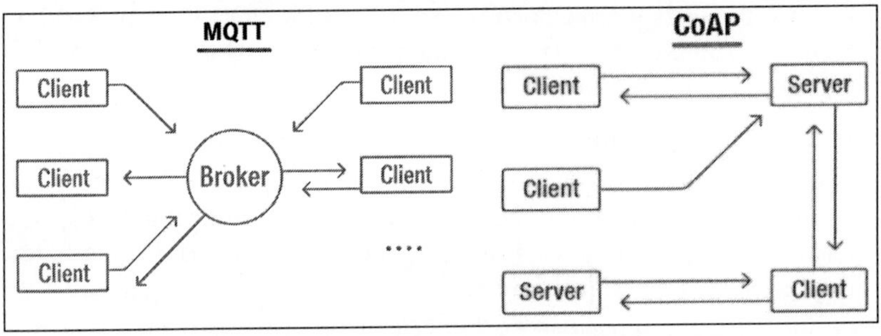

Fig. 3.25

IPV6 networking in Low power Personal Area Network(6LOWPAN)

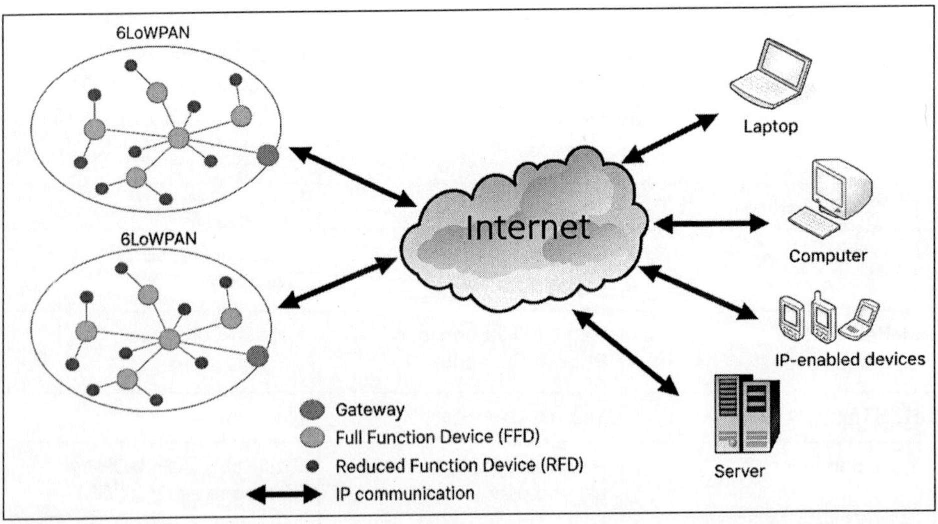

Fig. 3.26

It is an Internet Engineering Task Force (IETF), defined protocol that provides connectivity between wireless sensor networks and internet providing support to IPv6 using IEEE 802.15.4. It denotes a wireless link for low power personal area networks (LoWPANs). These networks are categorized by their more restricted abilities than other WPANs (e.g. Bluetooth) and WLANs (e.g.WiFi), they have small frame size, low data rate, low bandwidth, and low transmit power. 6LoWPAN is a simple low-cost communication network that allows wireless connectivity in applications with limited power and relaxed throughput requirements as it provides IPv6 networking over IEEE 802.15.4 networks. It is formed bydevices that are compatible with the IEEE 802.15.4 standard and characterized by short range, low bitrate, low power, low memory usage and low cost. When a lower processing capability sensor node in a6LoWPAN or so-called reduced function device (RFD) wants to send its data packet to an IP-enabled device outside the 6LoWPAN, it first sends the packet to the higher processing capability sensor nodeor so-called full function device (FFD) in the same PAN. The FFDs which react as a router in 6LoWPAN will forward the data packet hop by hop to the 6LoWPAN gateway. The 6LoWPAN gateway that connect to the 6LoWPAN with the IPv6 domain will then forward the packet to the destination IP-enabled device by using the IP address.

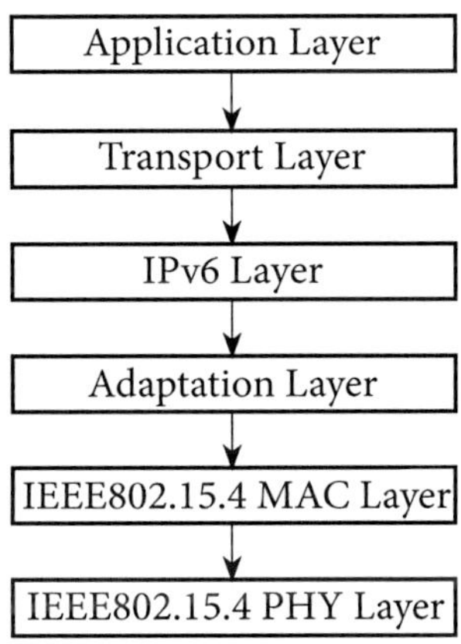

Fig. 3.27: The reference model of 6LoWPAN protocol stack.

It adopts IEEE 802.15.4 standard PHY and MAC layers as its bottom layers while chooses IPv6 in itsnetwork layer. Basically, IEEE 802.15.4 standard specifies PHY and MAC layers for low-rate wirelesspersonal area network (LR-WPAN). The PHY layer specification dictates how the IEEE 802.15.4 devices may communicate with each other over a wireless channel. There are total of 27 channels defined in the PHY layer. At MAC layer, it specifies when the devices may access the channel for communication. The basic tasks provided by the MAC layer are beacon generation and synchronization, supporting PAN association and disassociation, managing channel access via Carriers Sense Multiple Access with Collision Avoidance (CSMA/CA) mechanism, and etc. IEEE 802.15.4 standard defined 4frame structures for MAC layer: beacon frame, data frame, acknowledgement frame and MAC command frame. A beacon frame is used by a PAN coordinator to transmit beacons while a data frame is used fordata transfers. For the acknowledgement frame and the MAC command frame, they are used for confirming successful frame reception and handling all MAC peer entity control transfers respectively. Except acknowledgement frame which do not have MAC Service Data Unit (MSDU), other frames have the MSDU which is prefixed with a MAC Header (MHR) and appended with a MAC Footer (MFR). The MHR comprises frame control, sequence number and address information fields while the MSDUis the MAC payload of variable length that contains the information of IPv6 packet. The MFR contains Frame Check Sequence (FCS). The MAC frame that generally formed by MHR, MSDU and MFR is then passed to the PHY as a PHY payload. The PHY payload that acts as a PHY Service Data Unit (PSDU) in a PHY frame is prefixed by a synchronization header (SHR) and a PHY header (PHR). TheSHR contains the preamble and start-of-frame delimiter (SFD) fields that enable the receiver to synchronize and lock into the bit stream while the PHR contains frame length information.

6LoWPAN Meaning

IPv6 over Low power Wireless Personal Area Networks[11].

- **6 in 6LoWPAN:** The 6 is used because it is based on IPv6. IPv6 is the new Internet Protocol. IPv6 has replaced IPv4, because IPv4 runs out of address range. IPv4 offers 232 = 4,294,967,296 IP addresses inthe Internet. IPv6 uses 128-bit addresses, so the new address space supports 2128 = 3.4×1038addresses.
- **Lo in 6LoWPAN:** Lo represents Low Power. IP interchanges and Low Power utilization is generallyopposite. Furthermore 30 years prior our reality was not excessively green all things considered at present. We endeavor to spare power as regularly we can. At any rate, we do spare power since we might want to be green. We need to spare power on the grounds that the sensors are remote on battery control.
- **WPAN in 6LoWPAN:** WPAN represents Wireless Personal Area Networks. A WPAN is an individual region arrange for associating gadgets around an individual. A famous WPAN is Bluetooth. Bluetooth is being used to interconnect our PC frill or our sound hardware like Bluetooth headset or hands free unit. 6LoWPAN is more. In 6LoWPAN you can make fit systems with higher separation. By utilizing868/915 MHz rather than 2400 MHz the inclusion in structures is vastly improved.

6LoWPAN Protocol Stack

The 6LoWPAN technique is built on the IP protocol since IP is very suitable. One advantage is that IP isworld wide spread and computer engineers are already familiar with it. It means that less introduction is needed and the technology can be established faster than with a different set of protocols. But between the network layer and the data link layer, an adaption layer is placed. The adaption layer is embedded in the network layer.

Transport Layer

The transport layer protocol most preferably used for 6LoWPAN is UDP (User Datagram Protocol). It is lightweight (the full specification fits in two pages) and connectionless, which means that the two communicating processes do not have a standing connection established.

The UDP packages are called datagrams, and since there is no established connection between the processes, the address to the destination process must be attached to every datagram. UDP leaves no guarantee that they will reach their destination, or that they will reach it in thesame order as they were sent. This is the price for the lightweight; a quality that usually has ahigher priority for 6LoWPAN applications then reliability. The UDP header consists of 8 bytesand contains four fields of 16 bits each. For comparison, another common transport protocol from the IP stack called TCP (Transmission

Control Protocol) has a 20 bytes long header. Therefore is not as suitable for 6LoWPAN as UDP is.

Network Layer

The Network layer in the 6LoWPAN stack consists of the IPv6 Protocol. IPv6 was developed decades ago when the addresses of IPv4 (Internet protocol version 4) were predicted to run out. IPv4 has 32 bit-addresses which suffices to only 4 * 109 unique addresses. With the growing amount of Internet-connectable devices, it was not enough. Therefore, IPv6 was created with 128 bit addresses. That results in approximately 1038 addresses, which is "enough for every grain of sand on the planet" . The adaption layer is what makes IPv6 manageable for6LoWPAN. It compresses the IPv6 and UDP headers between the Edge Router and the node.This is possible since the Ipv6 prefix is no new information, since the IPv6 prefix address is shared between the Edge Router and all the nodes in a LoWPAN network. The Edge Router and the nodes only need to know each other's MAC addresses (Media Access Control address) toaddress each other.

Data link layer

The data link layer consists of the IEEE (Institute of Electrical and Electronics Engineers) 802.15.4, which is a link of low-power technology. 802.15.4 is used in many embedded applications, due to its small frame size and low bandwidth. It was designed to suit long livedapplications on low cost nodes, such as Smart Objects. 802.15.4 has a maximum packet size of127 bytes. With the 40 byte IPv6 header, this leaves less than 70 % of the packet for payload. This is the reason header compression is needed, so the IPv6 header only covers about 5 % ofthe packet and more can be used for payload . The link layer can be replaced by almost any other link radio frequency protocol. That is thanks to the great compatibility capacity of 6LoWPAN.

Features of 6LoWPAN

The main features of 6LoWPAN are as follows: It supports 64 bit or 16-bit addressing. It's specifically targeted at low power radios, one of them being Bluetooth low energy or Bluetooth smart standard andit takes advantage of header compression for IPv base and as well as for UDP headers. 6LoWPAN usesnetwork auto configuration for all participating devices, where each device is engaged in neighbor discovery. 6LoWPAN supports unicast, multicast, and broadcast and also the concept of fragmentation. The elementary size of a frame is 127 bytes taken from 15.4 standard and IPv6 transmission unit size is1280 bytes. One needs to fragment 1280 bytes into a set of 127 byte frames, which is supported by 6LoWPAN. 6LoWPAN also supports IP routing. It supports a link layer mesh networking and supportssecurity. Here the primary means of transport layer is UDP for 6LoWPAN. There is a specialized IPv6with LoWPAN and it uses 15.4 media access control and physical layers.

The adaptation layer is not only working with IPv6 protocol but it is used it IPv4 protocol. So, if we are use and network layer protocol with low power that's mean it is included in the adaptation layer. I am talking about IPv6 protocol that why call the 6lowpan. In 6lowpan do a header compression, fragmentation, reassembly, and decompression of header these four tasks are included. If we are working with the network layer then use the route over routing and if we are working with the adaptation layer then use the mesh under routing. 6lowpan has supported to the communication of any network. The data link layer is the detect and corrects the error which coming in the transmission of data bits. MAC is alsopresent in the data link layer. The data link layer senses the information with the use of the medium of collision transmission of the frame using a different protocol like CSMA/CD or CSMA/CA. adaptationlayer is also compression of the header like UDP, IPv6, ICMP, and also handles the fragmentation andreassembly process. In my work use the UDP protocol because TCP protocol is more complex compareto UDP. 6LOWPAN is using the application which needs to be real-time data with UDP protocol to getless complexity. For a security with UDP protocol use the DTLS it means datagram transport layer security protocol. In 6lowapn, COAP and MQTT protocols are used in the application layer.

3.9 DRONE TECHNOLOGY

A drone, also called an unmanned aerial vehicle (UAV), is a broad term that refers to an aircraft that operates autonomously or by remote control, with no pilot on board. Drones are usually small-or-medium-sized, and these 'flying robots' can carry out a wide range of tasks, from stealth military operations to package delivery to aerial photography. UAVs are often separated into two categories — civilian and military. While civilian UAVs are used for package deliveries and recreation, military drones are used for reconnaissance missions and aerial combat.

In order to fly, drones rely on a combination of hardware and software components. They are often equipped with rotors, propellers or fixed wings, sensors and cameras, navigation systems (GPS) and gyroscopes for stability.

Additionally, some of the most critical components of drone technology are its ground control station (GCS), payload and data links. Ground control stations are the hardware and software setups that allow drone operators to communicate with a drone from the ground. The GCS can be user controlled or operated via satellites. Drones are often capable of carrying payloads, which can range from life-saving medication to packages. Data links act as the transmission center that allow the drone to communicate with the ground operator while in flight.

The advent of 5G networks is transforming drone technology by enabling faster, more reliable communication between drones and control centers. 5G's high-speed data transmission allows for real-time video streaming, improving the accuracy of remote operations. In addition, 5G enhances long-distance control of drones, enabling them to operate in areas that are beyond the line of sight of their operators.

3.9.1 UAV System Architecture

Civilian UAV systems consist of three main elements, i.e., the unmanned aircraft, the ground control station (GCS), and the communication data link.

Flight controller: This is the central processing unit of the drone. In addition to stabilizing the drone during its course, this system reads the data provided by the sensors and processes it to extract useful information. According to different control commands, the controller either relays this information to the GCS or feeds the actuator control units directly with the current states. The flight controller implements the communication interface with the GCS. More precisely, commands from the GCS are processed by the flight controller, which in turn affects the deployed actuators. The flight controller can have multiple sensors integrated onboard or communicate with an external sensor unit. The UAV system can be equipped with various sensors including an accelerometer, gyroscope, magnetic orientation sensor, Global Positioning System (GPS) module and an electro-optical or infrared camera.

GCS: This is an on-land facility that provides the capabilities for human operators to control and/or monitor UAVs during their operations. GCSs vary in size according to the type and mission of the drones. In other words, for recreational mini and microdrones, GCSs are small handheld transmitters used by hobbyists. For tactical and strategic drones, a large self-contained facility with multiple workstations is employed as the GCS. A GCS communicates with the drone through a wireless link to send commands and receive real-time data, creating a virtual cockpit.

Data links: This is the wireless link used to carry control information between the drone and the GCS. The adopted communication link depends on the UAV operation range. According to their distance from the GCS, drone missions are categorized into line-of-sight (LOS) missions, where control signals can be sent and received via direct radio waves, and beyond lineof-sight (BLOS) missions, where the drone is controlled via satellite communications or a relaying aircraft that can be a drone itself.

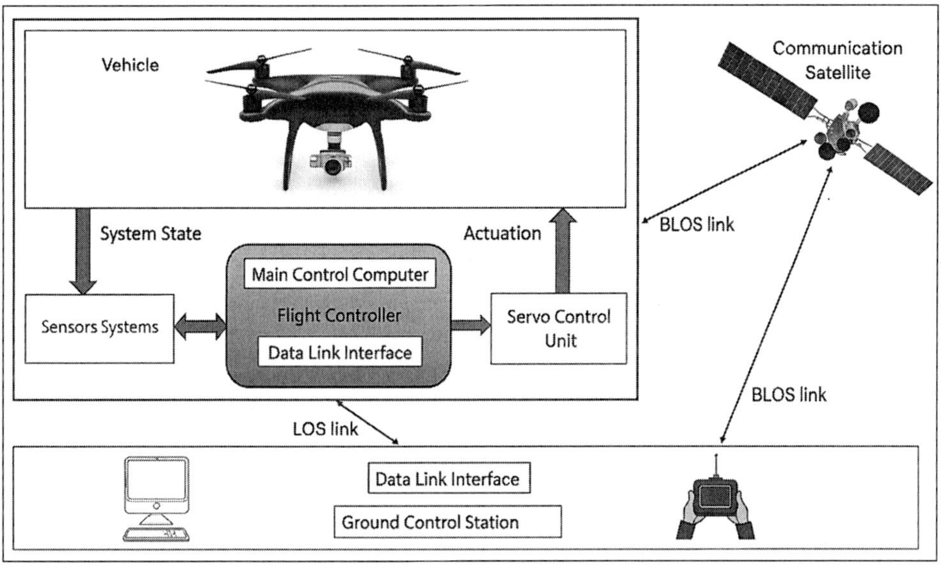

Fig. 3.28

3.9.2 Multi UAV Networks

Multi-UAV networks also known as Flying Ad-hoc Networks (FANETs) involve multiple Unmanned Aerial Vehicles (UAVs) or drones working together to form a network, working on a common goal offering enhanced capabilities for applications like surveillance, disaster response, and data collection, requiring coordination and efficient resource management. Multi-UAV systems can be controlled by a single operator or multiple interconnected operators. Key requirements of Multi UAVs are

- **Coordination:** UAVs must coordinate their actions, including trajectory planning, resource allocation, and data sharing.
- **Mobility:** UAVs are mobile and can move in three dimensions, creating a dynamic network topology.

- **Connectivity:** UAVs need to establish and maintain wireless communication links with each other and with ground infrastructure.

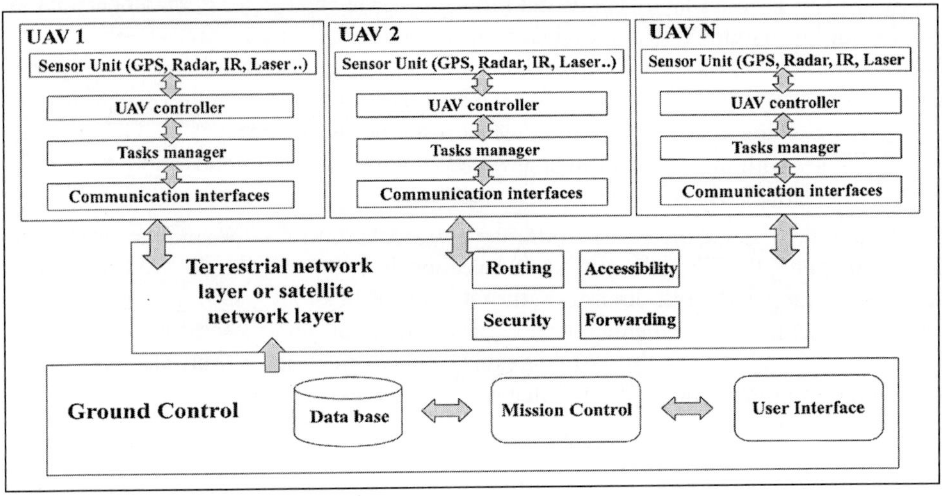

Fig. 3.29

These requirements can be met with the help of seamless communication through 5G.

3.9.3 Routing Protocols in Multi UAV

UAV networks have unique features and characteristics that are different from mobile ad hoc networks and vehicular ad hoc networks. The dynamic behavior of rapid mobility and topology changes in UAV networks makes the design of a routing protocol quite challenging. A routing protocol defines how drones communicate with each other and with a central control system to determine the best paths or routes for their movement from one location to another. These protocols are crucial for ensuring that UAVs can work together efficiently in multi-UAV systems. A routingalgorithm must consider the following aspects of the drone,

1. Path Planning

- A routing protocol helps drones decide the optimal path to follow, taking into account factors like flight distance, obstacles, and energy consumption.
- The goal is to minimize the overall cost (e.g., time, energy, risk) while ensuring that each UAV can avoid collisions and maintain effective communication with the others.

2. Communication and Data Exchange

- UAVs in a multi-UAV system need to share information such as location, battery status, and environmental conditions.
- Routing protocols facilitate communication between UAVs and ensure that the network of drones remains connected, even in dynamic or challenging environments like urban areas or forests.

3. Collision Avoidance

- Drones need to communicate and adjust their paths in real time to avoid collisions. Routing protocols enable dynamic updates to flight paths based on changes in the environment, such as the presence of new obstacles or the movement of other UAVs.

4. Dynamic Re-Routing

- If a drone encounters unexpected obstacles, interference, or failure of one of its components, routing protocols allow for dynamic re-routing of the drone to a safer or more optimal path.
- This feature is especially important in real-time applications such as search and rescue, where conditions change rapidly.

5. Energy Efficiency

- Drones have limited battery life, and efficient routing is crucial for conserving energy. Routing protocols help optimize paths based on energy consumption, ensuring that drones can complete their missions without running out of power mid-flight.

6. Network Topology

- In a multi-UAV system, the drones form a network with specific topologies (e.g., mesh networks). The routing protocol helps define how information flows between drones and the central control system.
- The topology can be dynamic, with drones joining or leaving the network, so the protocol needs to adjust accordingly.

3.9.4 Types of Routing Protocols in UAV Networks

1. Proactive Routing Protocols

- These protocols continuously update and maintain routes before they are needed. UAVs keep track of the entire network's topology, ensuring that the path to each destination is always available, even if the destination UAV is far away.
- **Example:** OLSR (Optimized Link State Routing) Protocol.

2. Reactive Routing Protocols

- These protocols establish routes only when a UAV needs to send data. The route is discovered on-demand, and no constant maintenance of network topology is required.
- **Example:** AODV (Ad hoc On-Demand Distance Vector) Protocol.

3. Hybrid Routing Protocols

- These protocols combine aspects of both proactive and reactive approaches. They may maintain some routes proactively and establish others reactively, depending on the needs of the system.
- **Example:** ZRP (Zone Routing Protocol).

4. Geographic Routing Protocols

- These protocols use geographic information such as the UAV's GPS coordinates to make routing decisions. Drones navigate based on their physical location, and routes are planned accordingly.
- **Example:** GPSR (Geographic Routing Protocol).

5. Swarm-Based Routing Protocols

- These protocols are inspired by swarm intelligence and decentralized decision-making, where UAVs collaborate with each other to find and follow the best routes based on local information, similar to how bees or ants work together in nature.
- **Example:** Ant Colony Optimization for UAV routing.

3.9.5 Applications Of Civilian Drones

1. Aerial Photography and Videography

Various drones are equipped with high-resolution cameras to capture aerial photos and videos. They are used in various industries such as filmmaking, real estate, tourism, and journalism to provide high-quality visual content.

2. Mapping and Surveying

Various drones are equipped with sensors such as LIDAR, and geometry cameras for creating detailed maps, 3D maps, and topographic surveys of terrains, and archaeological sites. They are valuable tools in urban planning and construction.

3. Agriculture

Drones are also used to perform agricultural activities such as crop monitoring, field mapping, pest detection, crop spraying, and precision irrigation.

4. Delivery Services

Delivery drones are being developed by various companies such as Amazon, UPS, and DHL to deliver goods from their warehouse to the customer's doorsteps. They offer faster delivery at a lower cost.

5. Security and Surveillance

Various drones are employed for surveillance, crowd monitoring, and security patrols in various areas such as airports, stadiums, industrial infrastructure, and public events. They provide support to security personnel in monitoring and enhancing situational awareness, deterring unauthorized activities.

3.9.6 Applications of Military Drones

Military drones, also known as Unmanned Combat Aerial Vehicles (UCAVs), are used for a wide range of applications, including intelligence, surveillance, target acquisition, reconnaissance, and even combat operations.

1. Search and Rescue

Various drones are equipped with thermal cameras, specialized sensors, and GPS systems used in search and rescue operations in disaster zones, wild zones, and urban areas. They provide aerial photos, and real-time situational awareness, and help rescue teams complete missions.

2. ISR (Intelligence, Surveillance, and Reconnaissance)

Drones use high-res cameras, infrared sensors, and other reconnaissance technologies to observe the enemy. The drones can move and seek out or sit above positions, feeding real-time imagery or other data to command units. These electric drones are useful for situational awareness, intelligence gathering, target acquisition, and battle damage assessment.

3. Combat

Limited by size, payloads may not be large guided missiles but modified grenades, mortar, or RPG rounds that are dropped on enemies below. The drone itself may also become a guided weapon when used as a "suicide drone" and driven, with its payload, into enemy vehicles or artillery.

3.9.7 Micro UAVs

A micro UAV (Unmanned Aerial Vehicle) refers to a very small drone, typically weighing less than 250 grams (or about 0.55 pounds). These tiny UAVs are designed for a wide range of applications, from hobbyist use to professional tasks, and they offer unique advantages and challenges due to their small size.

Characteristics of Micro UAVs

1. Size and Weight

- Micro UAVs are generally compact, lightweight, and portable. Their small size makes them easy to deploy in tight or confined spaces, and they can be highly maneuverable in various environments.

2. Flight Time and Range

- Due to their small size and limited battery capacity, micro UAVs typically have shorter flight times and smaller operational ranges compared to larger drones.
- Flight times are often in the range of 10-30 minutes, depending on the drone's design and battery efficiency.

3. Cost

- Micro UAVs are often more affordable compared to larger drones, making them an accessible option for enthusiasts, researchers, and small-scale commercial applications.

4. Sensors and Payloads

- Because of their small size, micro UAVs usually have limited capacity to carry payloads (such as cameras, sensors, or other equipment).
- However, many are equipped with high-quality cameras for photography or video recording, and some can carry light sensors for specific tasks like environmental monitoring or mapping.

5. Autonomy and Control

- Micro UAVs can be either manually controlled via remote control or autonomous, depending on the technology. Many models use GPS, vision-based navigation, or other sensors to navigate and avoid obstacles.
- Autonomous systems might use AI and machine learning algorithms to perform tasks without much human intervention.

6. Applications Micro UAVs are used in a variety of fields, including

- **Aerial Photography and Videography:** Micro UAVs are widely used for capturing images or videos in tight spaces, such as indoor environments, small outdoor areas, or urban locations.

- **Surveillance:** They are used for surveillance in areas where larger UAVs cannot fly, such as confined spaces or for inspecting small structures like bridges, rooftops, or power lines.
- **Search and Rescue:** Micro UAVs can be deployed in rescue operations in difficult-to-reach places, including through rubble or small spaces in disaster scenarios.
- **Environmental Monitoring:** They are used in applications like wildlife monitoring or collecting environmental data in areas that are hard to access with larger UAVs.
- **Inspection:** They can inspect small or intricate structures (e.g., pipelines, electrical equipment) where larger drones might not fit or be too cumbersome.
- **Hobby and Recreation:** Many enthusiasts use micro UAVs for personal drone flying and racing.

7. Advantages of Micro UAVs

- **Portability:** Micro UAVs are highly portable and easy to carry around, making them ideal for quick deployment.
- **Accessibility:** They are cheaper and easier to operate, making them an excellent choice for amateur drone users or businesses that need cost-effective solutions.
- **Maneuverability:** Their small size allows for highly agile flight and makes them ideal for flying in tight or cluttered environments.

8. Limitations of Micro UAVs

- **Limited Payload Capacity:** Micro UAVs can carry only lightweight cameras or sensors, which limits their ability to perform complex tasks requiring heavier equipment.
- **Limited Battery Life:** Due to their small size, their battery life is generally shorter, and their flight range is constrained.
- **Vulnerability to Weather:** Because of their lightweight nature, micro UAVs are more susceptible to wind, rain, and other challenging weather conditions.
- **Regulations:** In some regions, micro UAVs are subject to regulations, such as no-fly zones, airspace restrictions, or weight limits, which may impact their operational flexibility.

Examples of Micro UAVs

1. **DJI Tello:** A small, affordable drone perfect for beginners and hobbyists, featuring a decent camera for aerial photography and a range of about 100 meters.
2. **Parrot Mambo:** A micro drone designed for both indoor and outdoor use, with capabilities for carrying small objects and a camera.
3. **Ryze Tech Tello:** This is another example of a lightweight drone designed for educational purposes and basic aerial photography, offering fun features like programming capability and flight stability.

3.10 VEHICLE TO EVERYTHING (V2X)

With the rise in the number of connected cars, autonomous driving, and 5G connectivity, the future of Connected Vehicle Technology (CVT) has opened new dimensions in the way: vehicles, infrastructure, and pedestrians communicate with each other. This type of communication, which is essentially wireless between vehicles and its surroundings (including vehicles, pedestrians, devices, infrastructure, grid, and smart homes), is termed as Vehicle to everything (V2X). Vehicle to Everything (V2X) services is a direct or sidelink connections between vehicles (Vehicle-to-Vehicle, V2V) or between vehicles and infrastructure nodes (Vehicle-to-Infrastructure, V2I). Connections through the cellular network (Vehicle-to-Network, V2N) are usually envisioned for infotainment, comfort, or traffic management services. Connections of Vehicle-to-pedestrian (V2P) is established to alert the pedestrians about the vehicle movements. Though dedicated short range communication (DSRC) has been considered as the primary communication option for CVT safety applications, the use of other wireless technologies (e.g., Wi-Fi, LTE, WiMAX) allow longer range communications and throughput requirements that could not be supported by DSRC alone. Further, the use of other wireless technology potentially reduces the need for costly DSRC infrastructure. Hence 5g communications comes to V2X connectivity.

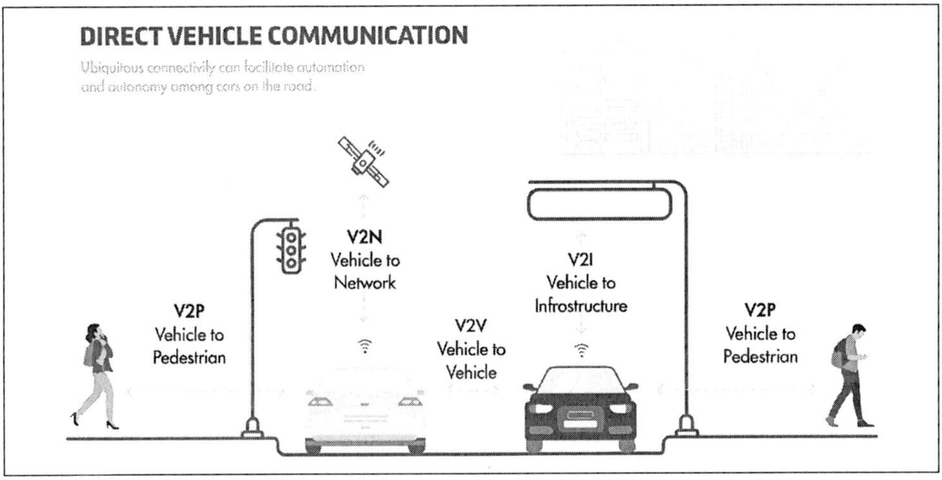

Fig. 3.30

3.10.1 The Architecture of V2X Communication

The principal objective of V2X communication is to establish communication between vehicles and their surroundings by combining hardware and software elements to improve traffic efficiency, road safety, and the overall driving experience.

Onboard Unit (OBU)

The OBU functions as an essential car communication hub. It enables wireless connections with other vehicles, roadside units (RSUs), buildings, and even pedestrians. It is equipped with sensors, processors, GPS, and a separate V2X communication module.

The external hardware components of the OBU include:

- A 4G/5G cellular modem that connects the V2N network to the outside world. The modem connects to the OBU through an mPCI adapter.
- A GPS/GNSS receiver that establishes the real-time positioning of the vehicle. It simultaneously allows the OBU to use Network Time Protocol (NTP) to run a GPS-based time service using the GPS-PPS signal.

- A Controller Area Network (CAN) bus to USB adapter connects to the in-vehicle sensors and actuators network. At the same time, the components of the OBU receive a constant power source from the DC/DC converter.
- All of the OBU's components receive a constant power source from the DC/DC converter.

An OBU can be used for diagnostic and emergency data storage, route planning, and navigation.

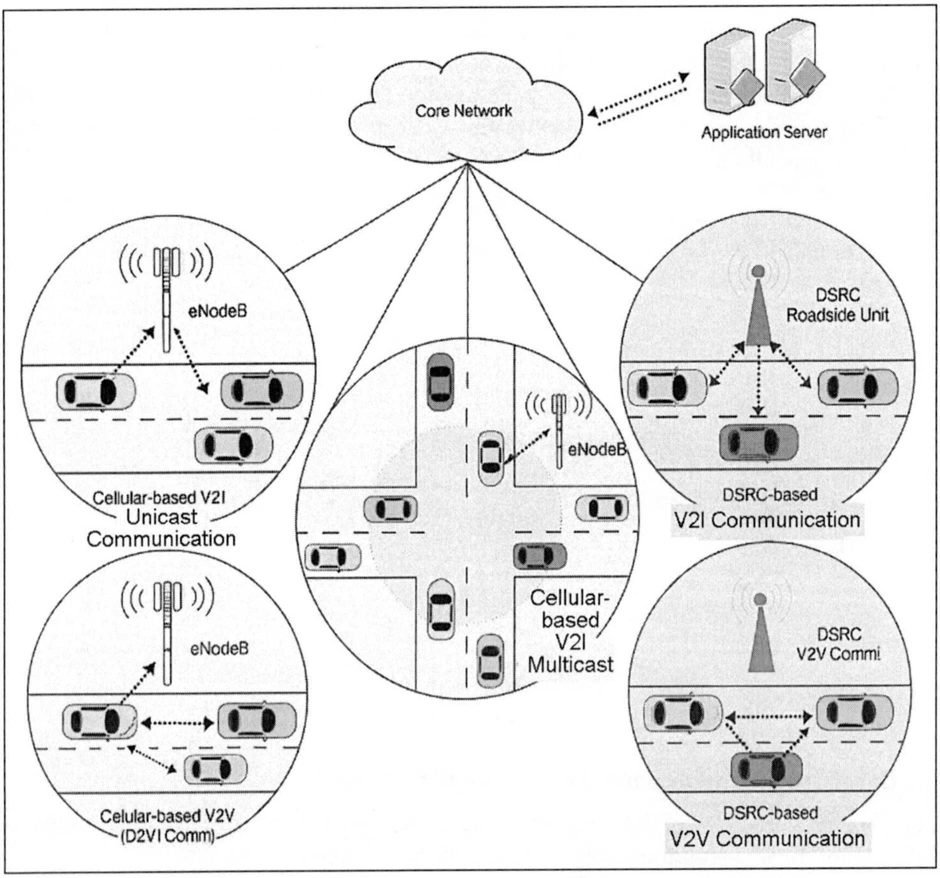

Fig. 3.31: A heterogenous vehicular networking architechture.

Roadside Unit (RSU)

An RSU (roadside unit) is a transceiver fixed to a road or pedestrian walkway, acting as a bridge between vehicles and transportation infrastructure. The RSU broadcasts and exchanges data to Onboard Units (OBUs) within its communications zone. If necessary, an RSU can also give operating instructions and channel assignments to the onboard Units. An RSU has two essential functions: streamlining traffic and improving safety.

The external hardware components of RSU include:

- Communication unit. (sensors such as LiDAR systems, and cameras,) and global navigation system satellite (GNSS).

- Edge computing node.
- Power supply.

3.10.2 Applications of V2X

Automotive Surrounding Sensing with GHz and THz Signals in V2X (Vehicle-to-Everything) refers to the use of advanced wireless communication and sensing technologies in vehicles to detect, perceive, and interact with their environment. This includes GHz (Gigahertz) and THz (Terahertz) signals for detecting obstacles, vehicles, pedestrians, and road conditions, as well as enabling V2X (Vehicle-to-Everything) communication between vehicles, infrastructure, and other elements of the transportation ecosystem. Some V2X applications include road safety, traffic management, and efficiency. The main objective of road safety applications is to reduce traffic collisions and improve awareness on the roads.

Intentionally left blank!

4

Quality of Service

Outcome

- 5G QoS Identifier (5QI)
- Network Slicing for QoS Customization
- Guaranteed vs. Non-Guaranteed Bit Rate (GBR vs. Non-GBR)
- Low Latency and High Reliability (URLLC)
- Dynamic QoS Adaptation and Traffic Prioritization

> 5G can dynamically adjust QoS based on contextual awareness, such as the user's movement, device type, and environmental conditions. For example, if a user is moving through a busy urban area or entering a crowded stadium, the 5G network can dynamically allocate more resources to that user for uninterrupted service, while still balancing the needs of others.
>
> **Interesting Fact**

Quality of Service (QoS) in 5G technology refers to the ability of a network to provide differentiated service levels based on the specific requirements of various applications and users. Unlike previous generations, 5G introduces a more advanced and flexible QoS framework that enables ultra-reliable, low-latency communications (URLLC), enhanced mobile broadband (eMBB), and massive machine-type communications (mMTC). These service categories require different network parameters such as latency, bandwidth, and reliability. To achieve this, 5G employs network slicing, which allows operators to create virtualized and isolated network segments tailored to specific use cases. Additionally, 5G leverages advanced traffic management techniques, including priority scheduling, dynamic resource allocation, and intelligent routing, to optimize performance. With these capabilities, 5G QoS ensures seamless connectivity for applications like autonomous vehicles, remote healthcare, industrial automation, and immersive media experiences, significantly improving user experience and service efficiency.

4.1 QUALITY OF SERVICE (QoS) ARCHITECTURE IN 5G

Quality of Service (QoS) in 5G networks ensures that different types of traffic receive the necessary priority, latency, and reliability. The 5G QoS framework is more flexible and granular compared to 4G, enabling efficient handling of diverse applications such as ultra-reliable low-latency communication (URLLC), enhanced mobile broadband (eMBB), and massive machine-type communication (mMTC).

Terms in Architecture diagram

- **PCF**: Defines QoS policies.
- **SMF**: Enforces QoS flows in PDU sessions.
- **UPF**: Implements QoS rules and forwards traffic.
- **QoS Flows**: Different services have different QoS requirements (e.g., voice vs. web browsing). **gNB**: Allocates radio resources efficiently.
- **UE (User Equipment)**: Receives data based on QoS priorities

```
+------------------------------------------------------+
|                5G QoS Architecture                   |
+------------------------------------------------------+
|             Policy Control Function (PCF)            |
|        (Manages QoS rules and policies)              |
+------------------------------------------------------+
                          |
                          ▼
+------------------------------------------------------+
|        Session Management Function (SMF)             |
|    (Assigns QoS flows and enforces rules)            |
+------------------------------------------------------+
                          |
                          ▼
+------------------------------------------------------+
|        User Plane Function (UPF)                     |
| (Traffic classification and QoS flow enforcement)    |
+------------------------------------------------------+
                          |
                          ▼
+-----------------------+        +-----------------------+
|  QoS Flow 1 (5QI-1)   |        |  QoS Flow 2 (5QI-9)   |
| (e.g., Voice Call)    |        | (e.g., Web Browsing)  |
+-----------------------+        +-----------------------+
                          |
                          ▼
+------------------------------------------------------+
|         gNB (5G Base Station)                        |
| (Manages Radio Bearers and Resource Allocation)      |
+------------------------------------------------------+
                          |
                          ▼
+------------------------------------------------------+
|        5G Device (UE)                                |
| (Receives traffic with different QoS priorities)     |
+------------------------------------------------------+
```

4.1.1 QoS Framework in 5G

5G QoS is built on a framework that includes key components such as QoS flows, 5G QoS Identifiers (5QI), and Policy Control.

Key Components

- **QoS Flow**: The fundamental unit of QoS in 5G, replacing the EPS bearer in 4G. Each flow is identified by a **QoS Flow Identifier (QFI)**.
- **5G QoS Identifier (5QI)**: A standardized identifier that defines QoS parameters like priority, packet delay budget, and packet error rate.

- **Session and Service Differentiation**: Unlike 4G, 5G allows multiple QoS flows within a single PDU (Packet Data Unit) session, making it more efficient.

4.1.2. QoS Flow and PDU Session Relationship

- A **PDU session** (similar to an EPS bearer in 4G) can carry multiple QoS flows.
- Each QoS flow can have different QoS requirements based on the service.
- QoS flows are mapped to **Data Radio Bearers (DRB)** for transmission over the radio interface.

4.1.3. QoS Parameters

Each 5QI is associated with specific QoS characteristics:

- **Resource Type**: Guaranteed Bit Rate (GBR) or Non-GBR.
- **Packet Delay Budget (PDB)**: Defines latency requirements.
- **Packet Error Rate (PER)**: Ensures reliability for different traffic types.
- **Priority Level**: Determines which traffic gets served first in congestion scenarios.

Examples of 5QI Mappings

5QI	Service Type	Packet Delay Budget	Packet Error Rate	Priority
1	Conversational Voice	100 ms	10^{-2}	2
2	Live Video Streaming	150 ms	10^{-3}	4
3	Real-time Gaming	50 ms	10^{-3}	3
9	Web Browsing, Video Streaming	300 ms	10^{-6}	9

4.1.4 QoS Control Mechanisms

a. Policy Control and Charging Function (PCF)

- The **PCF** defines QoS policies and rules based on user subscription, network conditions, and service requirements.
- It ensures that network resources are allocated based on business policies.

> **In a 5G environment, Mobile Virtual Network Operators (MVNOs) can have their own customized QoS profiles, even if they don't own the infrastructure.**
>
> *Interesting Fact*

b. User Plane Function (UPF)

- The **UPF** enforces QoS policies, marking and shaping traffic according to the assigned QoS flows.
- It supports **flow-based QoS management** by forwarding traffic according to the defined QoS rules.

c. Radio Resource Management (RRM)

- The **gNB (Next Generation NodeB)** performs **radio scheduling**, ensuring that different QoS flows get the required bandwidth and latency.

4.1.5 QoS Differentiation for 5G Services

5G supports multiple service categories, each with different QoS needs:

- **eMBB (Enhanced Mobile Broadband)**: Requires high data rates with moderate latency.
- **URLLC (Ultra-Reliable Low Latency Communication)**: Demands very low latency (<1ms) and high reliability (10^{-5} packet loss).
- **mMTC (Massive Machine-Type Communication)**: Supports a large number of low-power devices with relaxed QoS requirements.

4.1.6. Dynamic QoS Adaptation

5G networks use **Network Slicing** to create virtual network partitions with specific QoS characteristics. This allows:

- A dedicated slice for ultra-low latency applications.
- A slice optimized for high-bandwidth applications.
- A slice for massive IoT connectivity with low data rates.

The 5G QoS architecture introduces a **more flexible and efficient framework** compared to 4G, allowing precise control over traffic flows and meeting the diverse demands of new applications. By leveraging **QoS flows, 5QI, policy control, and network slicing**, 5G ensures optimal performance for a wide range of use cases.

4.2 QoS ATTRIBUTES IN 5G

Quality of Service (QoS) in 5G is defined by several key attributes that determine how network resources are allocated and managed for different services. These attributes ensure that applications with different requirements—such as ultra-low latency gaming, high-bandwidth streaming, and massive IoT—receive the appropriate network treatment.

> In 5G networks, security mechanisms can impact Quality of Service (QoS), as the implementation of advanced encryption and authentication protocols can introduce additional latency and processing overhead. However, by optimizing security processes and integrating them into the QoS management framework, operators can ensure that services maintain high levels of security without significantly compromising performance, especially for sensitive applications like financial transactions or healthcare services.
>
> **Interesting Fact**

4.2.1 Key QoS Attributes in 5G

a. 5G QoS Identifier (5QI)

- Each QoS flow is assigned a **5QI**, which maps to predefined QoS characteristics.
- It determines how packets are prioritized, their delay budget, and reliability requirements.

b. Resource Type

- **Guaranteed Bit Rate (GBR):** Ensures a minimum data rate for applications like video conferencing.

- **Non-GBR:** No strict data rate guarantee, suitable for applications like web browsing.

c. Packet Delay Budget (PDB)

- Specifies the maximum delay tolerated by a QoS flow.
- Low PDB (e.g., 1ms) is critical for URLLC applications like autonomous driving.
- Higher PDB (e.g., 300ms) is acceptable for non-real-time services.

d. Packet Error Rate (PER)

- Defines the acceptable packet loss probability.
- **URLLC services** require extremely low PER (~10^{-5}) for high reliability.
- **Streaming applications** can tolerate slightly higher PER.

e. Priority Level

- Determines the order in which packets are processed during congestion.
- Lower numerical values represent **higher priority**.
- Example: Voice calls (5QI-1) have **higher priority** than file downloads (5QI-9).

4.2.2. QoS Parameter Table (Example)

5QI	Service Type	Resource Type	Packet Delay Budget	Packet Error Rate	Priority Level
1	Conversational Voice	GBR	100 ms	10^{-2}	2
2	Real-time Video	GBR	150 ms	10^{-3}	4
3	Gaming	GBR	50 ms	10^{-3}	3
5	V2X Communication	GBR	10 ms	10^{-5}	1
9	Web Browsing	Non-GBR	300 ms	10^{-6}	9

4.2.3. QoS Enforcement in 5G

a. Policy and Charging Rules Function (PCF)

- Defines QoS rules based on user subscriptions and network policies.

b. Session Management Function (SMF)

- Assigns QoS flows and ensures compliance with network policies.

c. User Plane Function (UPF)

- Enforces QoS policies by prioritizing and shaping traffic accordingly.

4.2.4. Dynamic QoS Adaptation

- **Network Slicing**: Allocates separate QoS attributes for different services.
- **Adaptive QoS Scaling**: Adjusts QoS dynamically based on network conditions.

5G QoS attributes provide **granular control** over network traffic, ensuring each service gets the required bandwidth, latency, and reliability. These attributes play a crucial role in supporting applications from **autonomous vehicles** to **cloud gaming**.

4.3 3GPP in 5G: An Overview

3rd Generation Partnership Project (3GPP) is the global standards organization responsible for developing technical specifications for mobile communication systems, including **5G (5th Generation)** networks. It defines the architecture, protocols, and features that enable 5G to support high-speed, low-latency, and massive connectivity applications.

3GPP (3rd Generation Partnership Project) is an international collaboration of telecommunications organizations that develops standards for mobile networks. It was founded in **1998** to standardize **3G (UMTS)** and later expanded to 4G (LTE) and 5G.

3GPP consists of **regional standardization bodies**, including:

- ETSI (Europe)
- ATIS (North America)
- TSDSI (India)
- ARIB & TTC (Japan)
- CCSA (China)
- TTA (South Korea)

4.3.1 Role in 5G Standardization

a. 5G New Radio (5G NR)

- 3GPP defined **5G NR**, a new radio access technology optimized for ultra-fast speeds, low latency, and energy efficiency.
- Supports **FR1 (Sub-6 GHz)** and **FR2 (mmWave) frequency bands.**

> 5G New Radio (NR) uses a wide range of frequency bands—from sub-1 GHz frequencies (Low-Band) to mmWave frequencies (above 24 GHz), offering unprecedented flexibility in delivering ultra-fast speeds and low latency. This allows 5G to meet the diverse demands of different applications, from urban environments requiring high bandwidth (using mmWave) to rural areas needing broader coverage (using Low-Band).
>
> **Interesting Fact**

b. 5G Core Network (5GC)

- 3GPP introduced a **cloud-native, service-based architecture (SBA)** for 5G Core.
- Allows flexible deployment of network functions, enabling **network slicing** and **multi-access edge computing** (MEC).

c. 5G Network Slicing

- 3GPP defines **network slicing**, allowing operators to create virtual networks for different use cases (e.g., IoT, gaming, autonomous vehicles).

d. 5G Use Cases

- **cMBB (Enhanced Mobile Broadband)**: High-speed internet for 4K/8K streaming, VR, AR.

- **URLLC (Ultra-Reliable Low-Latency Communication)**: Critical applications like autonomous driving and remote surgery.
- **mMTC (Massive Machine-Type Communication)**: IoT applications with millions of low-power devices.

4.3.2 3GPP 5G Releases

3GPP develops 5G in phases, known as **Releases**:

3GPP Release	Key Features
Release 15 (2018)	First official 5G NR specification, NSA/SA architecture
Release 16 (2020)	Enhancements for URLLC, V2X, private networks, industrial IoT
Release 17 (2022)	IoT optimizations, satellite integration, 5G efficiency improvements
Release 18 (2024-2025)	5G-Advanced (AI/ML in networks, extended XR support)

4.3.3 3GPP Impacts 5G Networks

- **Ensures global compatibility**: Devices and networks follow the same technical standards worldwide.
- **Improves performance**: Optimized radio access and core network for better speed, latency, and reliability.
- **Enables innovation**: Supports futuristic applications like **metaverse, connected cars, and smart cities**.

3GPP plays a **critical role in defining 5G standards**, ensuring a **unified, scalable, and interoperable** global ecosystem. With **5G-Advanced (Release 18)** on the horizon, 3GPP continues to evolve 5G towards **6G and beyond**.

4.4 CHALLENGES OF QOS IN 5G NETWORKS

Ensuring Quality of Service (QoS) in 5G is challenging due to the complexity of network architecture, diverse use cases, and high-performance expectations. Below are some key challenges:

1. Ultra-Low Latency Requirements

- **Challenge:** Applications like autonomous vehicles, remote surgery, and industrial automation require ultra-low latency (~1ms).
- **Issue:** Maintaining this low latency is difficult due to network congestion, signal interference, and multi-hop transmissions.

2. High Mobility and Handover Issues

- **Challenge:** 5G networks must support high-speed mobility (e.g., 500 km/h for high-speed trains).
- **Issue:** Ensuring seamless handovers between cells while maintaining QoS for services like video calls and gaming is complex.

3. Network Slicing Complexity

- **Challenge:** 5G introduces network slicing to allocate dedicated resources for different services (e.g., IoT, broadband, mission-critical applications).
- **Issue:** Managing multiple slices dynamically while ensuring end-to-end QoS across different network components is difficult.

> Network slicing in 5G allows operators to create virtual, isolated networks tailored to specific use cases or customer needs. For example, one slice could be optimized for low latency and high reliability for autonomous vehicles, while another slice could be tailored for high-bandwidth applications like 4K video streaming, all running on the same physical infrastructure but operating independently.
>
> **Interesting Fact**

4. Congestion Control in High-Traffic Scenarios

- **Challenge:** 5G supports massive connectivity, handling millions of devices per square kilometer (mMTC).
- **Issue:** High traffic loads in smart cities, stadiums, and dense urban areas can lead to congestion, affecting QoS for critical applications.

5. Security and QoS Interdependencies

- **Challenge:** 5G must secure network slices, user data, and signaling while maintaining QoS.
- **Issue:** Encryption and security protocols add overhead, impacting latency and throughput.

6. Edge Computing and QoS Management

- **Challenge:** 5G integrates Multi-access Edge Computing (MEC) for low-latency processing.
- **Issue:** Balancing workload distribution between the cloud and edge servers while maintaining QoS is complex.

7. Packet Loss and Jitter in mmWave Networks

- **Challenge:** 5G uses mmWave frequencies (FR2) for high-speed data.
- Issue: Signal attenuation, blockage (by walls, trees, rain), and interference lead to packet loss and jitter, affecting real-time applications.

8. Regulatory and Spectrum Allocation Issues

- **Challenge:** 5G requires a variety of spectrum bands (low, mid, and high frequencies).
- **Issue:** Limited spectrum availability and regulatory constraints impact QoS, especially in developing regions.

Ensuring QoS in 5G is a multidimensional challenge, requiring optimized resource allocation, dynamic traffic management, and advanced AI-based network optimization. Future enhancements in 6G may address some of these limitations with better spectrum efficiency, AI-driven automation, and quantum communication.

TEACHERS KNOW MORE

- In 5G, autonomous vehicles benefit from ultra-reliable low-latency communication (URLLC), which is part of the QoS framework designed specifically for safety-critical applications.
- 5G can dynamically adjust QoS based on contextual awareness, such as the user's movement, device type, and environmental conditions.
- In a 5G environment, Mobile Virtual Network Operators (MVNOs) can have their own customized QoS profiles, even if they don't own the infrastructure.
- 5G offers sub-meter level accuracy for location-based services, which is leveraged to manage QoS in environments like smart cities and industrial automation.
- For VR applications, 5G enables a dedicated QoS profile that minimizes jitter and guarantees ultra-low latency, ensuring that users experience seamless, immersive environments.
- 5G allows for mission-critical QoS tailored for first responders, law enforcement, and public safety networks, ensuring prioritized access during emergencies.
- 5G's energy efficiency is an often-overlooked part of its QoS framework. 5G uses advanced sleep modes and intelligent resource management to optimize power consumption.
- Low-power, wide-area networks (LPWANs) in 5G support low bandwidth IoT devices (like smart meters, agricultural sensors) that operate with low data requirements but need a high level of reliability and long-range communication.
- 5G incorporates advanced interference management techniques that adjust QoS in real-time to prevent network congestion and optimize signal clarity.
- 5G can push QoS to the edge of the network, allowing real-time processing of applications without needing to route data back to a central server.
- 5G is built to support heterogeneous networks (HetNets), which use a combination of macro, small, and micro cells to improve coverage and capacity.

Intentionally left blank!